T0159100

Angels and Spirits

DR. JOHN THOMAS WYLIE

authorHOUSE®

AuthorHouse™
1663 Liberty Drive
Bloomington, IN 47403
www.authorhouse.com
Phone: 1 (800) 839-8640

Published by AuthorHouse 01/11/2019

ISBN: 978-1-5462-7567-1 (sc)
ISBN: 978-1-5462-7566-4 (e)

Contents

CHAPTER TWO

CHAPTER THREE

CHAPTER FOUR

CHAPTER FIVE

CHAPTER SIX

CHAPTER SEVEN

Introduction

IN THIS PUBLICATION, "ANGELS And Spirits," the Scripture teaches that there is an order of intelligences higher than that of men; and further asserts that these intelligences are connected with man in providence and in the redemptive economy. These intelligences are called "Spirits" to denote their specific role and nature; they are called "Angels" to denote their mission. We will investigate their involvement with mankind and their tasks. Nothing can be known of them other than that which is revealed in the Scriptures. They are created spirits but the time of their creation is not indicated. Many Biblical Scholars hold that such a creation must have been included in the statement found in Genesis 1:1, and therefore preceding the six days' formative period.

God alone, is pure, essential Spirit; these created spirits are clothed with ethereal vestures, such as Paul describes when he says, "There is a spiritual body (I Cor. 15:44). Thus our Lord tell us the children of the resurrection are, equal unto the angels (Luke 20:36). Having a more subtle organization than man, they are at present higher in their range of faculties; greater in power and might (II Peter 2:11), and angels that excel in strength (Psalm 103:20) (Christian Theology, H.O. Wiley, 1940).

The highest exercise of angels is to wait upon God. Their chief duty is to minister to the heirs of salvation. As we embark upon this reading, my hope is that you will come to take seriously the informative topics presented to you. We do not intend to dwell on Satan or his angels too much (only as necessary), but focus on the deeds and tasks of holy angels.

Reverend Dr. John Thomas Wylie

The Ministry Of Angels

THE MOST NOTEWORTHY EXERCISE of holy messengers (angels) is to hold up upon God. The articulation, :Lord of hosts," alludes to the Lord gone to by His holy messengers (angels). When it is said that every one of the children of God shouted for joy (Job 38:7) the reference is to the blessed messengers (angels) as sons. Their main obligation is to minister to the heirs of salvation.

They were present at creation, at the giving of the law, at the introduction of Christ, after the temptation in the wilderness, in Gethsemane, at the resurrection and the ascension. Thus the creator of Hebrews asks, Are they not all ministering spirits, sent forward to minister for them who will be heirs of salvation? (Heb. 1:14).

Heavenly attendants (angels) are partitioned into three progressive systems or hierarchies: (1) Thrones, cherubim and seraphim who go immediately upon God; (2) Dominions, virtues and powers, which worked in nature and in warfare; and (3) Principalities, archangels and blessed messengers (angels), which fulfilled special missions and ministered to the heirs of salvation (Christian Theology, Wiley, O.H. 1940).

Good And Evil Angels

THE HEAVENLY ATTENDANTS (ANGELS) in their unique domain were sacred creatures, supplied with opportunity of will and exposed to a time of probation. They were intended to pick willfully the administration of God, and in this way be set up for the free administration of ministering to the heirs of salvation. They didn't all keep their first estate, yet some fell into transgression and rebellion to God.

Consequently, we read of the judgment of the fallen angel (I Tim. 3:6) who we assemble from the Scriptures was at the leader of that portion of the blessed messengers (angels) which fell away. Satan therefore is known as the "prince of the power of the air" (Eph. 2:2), and his hosts are alluded to as spiritual wickedness in high places (Eph. 6:12).

We may accept additionally that following their trial period, the great heavenly attendants (angels) were affirmed in holiness and confirmed to a condition of glory a condition of indefectibility wherein they generally see the face of God (Matt. 18:10). The wicked in like manner were confirmed in the condition of wickedness, misery. Their fall was not because of any need from inside, or any impulse from without, but might be viewed as intentional abandonment, voluntary apostasy.

It is construed that their wrongdoing (sin) was pride (I Tim. 3:6). As a result of their sin they have been brought under the judgment and condemnation of God (II Peter 2:4), and will be punished eternally (Matt. 25:41). Since God is a God of love, we may infer that this portion of angels were not salvable, or He would have made provision for their salvation.

Their disposition toward God is one of hostility, this dangerous intention being focused in Satan who stands at their head.

Satan

SATAN IS A PERSONAL being, the leader of the kingdom of malice, evil spirits (fallen messengers, angels). He is the basic enemy of Christ and man. Two names primarily, are connected to him, the two of which express his character. He is Satan, or enemy, and fiend (diabolus) or calumniator. Our Lord portrays him as sowing the seeds of blunder and uncertainty in the Church (Matt. 13:39), and as being both a liar and a killer (John 8:44). He is capable likewise to change himself into a blessed messenger of light. Satan is a personal being.

Chapter
ONE

Angels In The Bible

The Archangel Michael

MICHAEL WHO IS GENUINELY critical is the archangel (which means a sort of "over or head over every single other holy angel). The prophet Daniel alluded to him as "a prince," kind of protector or grand defender of Israel (Daniel 10:13,21; 12:1). The book of Revelation pictures a contention toward the end of time, with Michael and his heavenly attendants (angels) battling against the winged serpent, Lucifer, or best known as Satan (12:7).

Michael is one of two holy messengers with names in the Bible, the other being Gabriel.

While the Bible notices his name just five times, Jewish and Christian legends had much to say in regards to Michael. Jewish custom says that he was the strange "man" who grappled with Jacob, that he passed on the Law to Moses on Sinai, that he assumed a job in the wonderful risings of Enoch and Elijah, that he was the seraph who contacted Isaiah's lips with a live coal, and that he replaced the insubordinate Lucifer (Satan) as pioneer of the heavenly choirs.

The Angel Gabriel

GABRIEL ASSUMES A JOB in the narrative of Jesus' introduction to the world and the introduction of His brother John the Baptist. Luke 1 recounts the cleric Zechariah, who saw the holy messenger in the temple. Gabriel declared that Zechariah's wife, Elizabeth, would bear a child who might "make prepared a people arranged for the Lord" (1:17). Zechariah, who was old, had questions, and Gabriel, who said he remained "within the sight of God," rebuffed Zechariah with muteness till the birth happened.

Gabriel went to Mary in Nazareth and revealed to her she was to bear a child, "the child of the Highest" (Luke 1:32). Mary said she was a virgin, but Gabriel advised her, "The Holy Spirit will happen upon you, and the intensity of the Highest will dominate you; along these lines, likewise, that Holy One who is to be conceived will be known as the Son of God" (Luke 1:35).

Gabriel shows up in the book of Daniel as a mediator of Daniel's baffling dreams (8:16; 9:21), and as one who conceded Daniel insight and comprehension.

Between the Old and New Testaments, numerous legends about Gabriel came to fruition.

An Old Christian convention has it that Gabriel will blow the trumpet to flag the apocalypse, yet the Bible does not make reference to his name in this association.

The Old Testament

"Let Us Make Man"

In Genesis 1, the high purpose of God's formation of all things was the making of man. On the 6th day, in the wake of making every one of the creatures, God stated, "Let us make man in our picture, in our resemblance" (1:26). Ages of Bible perusers have made the undeniable inquiry: Who is this "us," since God is the "Only" God? This has kept the researchers occupied.

In any case, the basic Hebrew name for God is "elohim," or, in other words. Christians trust that the plural pronoun reflects the Trinity-that is, the one God, yet in addition the Trinity of Father, Son, and Holy Spirit. Be that as it may, before Christianity the Jews saw another importance in "us" and "our": God was addressing the blessed angels, His heavenly court. Is this translation correct? Difficult to state. Unquestionably the Bible advances that the blessed angels were available when God made man (Ps. 8:5).

The signifying "our image" is by all accounts this: God has recently made creatures, yet man is exceptional, made to resemble God and like the heavenly attendants from multiple points of view.

When Were The Angels Created?

HOLY ANGELS ARE SPECIFIED in Genesis 1:1, however Psalm 148 alludes to their creation (however not to the time), thus does Colossians 1:16. Yet, it is obvious from the book of Job that they had just been made when God started making the earth, for God asked Job, "where were you when I established the frameworks of the earth?"... "When the morning stars sang together, and every one of the children of God yelled for delight?" (Job 38:4,7). It is for the most part concurred that the "morning stars" and the "children of God" were blessed angels.

Other than the Bible, the Jewish compositions known as the Book of Jubilees, composed between the Old and New Testaments, give data about the time the blessed messengers (angels) were made: It was the main day of Creation.

The Bible's First Angels

PEOPLE DEPENDABLY INTERFACE THE Garden of Eden with the seducer, Satan. In any case, there were angels associated with Eden also, however in no charming sense. After the serpent tempted Adam and Eve, they ate the forbidden fruit, and on the grounds that they disobeyed God, they were expelled from Eden. The portal of Eden was watched by cherubim (holy angel) and a blazing, flaming sword, a distinctive image that once man had sinned he would never return to Eden (Gen. 3:24).

The sons Of God

BOOK OF SCRIPTURES RESEARCHERS keep running into a few issues that just can't be comprehended. One is found in Genesis 6:1-4: "When men started to increase on the substance of the earth, and daughters of men, that they were beautiful... The children of God came in to the daughters of men and they bore children to them.

Those were the powerful men who were of old, men of prestige." Just who were the "sons of God" Angels? Fallen Angels? Evil spirits? Nobody knows without a doubt. Be that as it may, the broadly read book of Enoch, composed between the Old and New Testaments, expresses that the "sons of God" of Genesis 6 were fallen angels, whose association with human women created a wide range of evils on the earth.

Ishmael's Guardian

Ishmael was the son of Abraham and his mistress, Hagar. After he was conceived, Abraham's better half, Sarai, pushed mother and youngster away, however a heavenly angel saved them from dying (Gen. 16). The country of Israel was descended from Abraham's son Isaac, however Genesis records that an extraordinary country was plunged from Ishmael too. Middle Easterners follow their family line to Ishmael, called Ismail in the Koran, the Muslim's blessed book which says Ishmael was Abraham's most loved child, not Isaac.

Lot, His Wife, And Sodom

Lot, the nephew of Abraham, was the main inhabitant (and his family) of the evil city of Sodom that God saved. Genesis 19 recounts the despicable story of two celestial guests who were relatively assaulted (raped) by the men of Sodom. The guests encouraged Lot to escape the bound city. They fled, and God poured down fire on Sodom. The holy angels had advised the family not to think back, but rather Lot's better half did, and she turned into a mainstay of salt. (Jesus stated, "Remember Lot's wife" a notice not to think back on one's past).

Old Testament Trinity – Or Angels?

Genesis 18 relates that the Lord appeared to Abraham as he was sitting in his tent entryway. Be that as it may, "the Lord" showed up as three men. Abraham engaged them affably, and "He" (the Lord - which of the three men was talking?) anticipated that when He came back again later, Abraham's better half, Sarah, would have a child. Sarah listening close-by, giggled, since she and Abraham were both old. In any case, the prediction materialized, for she brought forth Isaac.

This passage of Scripture interests Bible perusers, since it alludes to "the Lord" and "He" but in addition demands that three men, not one, visited Abraham. Is it accurate to say that one was of the three men God in the flesh, while the other two blessed angels? A few perusers have recommended this was the Trinity - what the New Testament alludes to as God the Father, the Son, and the Holy Spirit. So maybe Abraham's guests were a sort of "Old Testament Trinity."

The Sacrifice Of Isaac

THIS IS A STANDOUT amongst the most touching stories in the Bible. Abraham at long last had a child, Isaac (as God had guaranteed), in his maturity (100 years of age). Yet, shockingly, God later told Abraham to "take now your child, your only child Isaac, whom you cherish (love), and go to the place that is known for Moriah, and offer him there as a consumed offering" (Gen. 22:2).

Abraham, the good example of trust in God, complied. The story relates that the child Isaac asked his father for what valid reason there were fire and wood yet no sheep for a sacrifice. Abraham replied, "God will provide" (Gen. 22:8). Abraham bound the child and raised his blade to slaughter him, however was ceased by a holy angel, who stated, "Don't lay your hand on the lad, or do anything to him; for the now I realize that you fear God" (Gen. 22:12). The holy angel said that in light of Abraham's faith God would most likely bless him.

Numerous old countries near Israel rehearsed child sacrifice. Israel dependably censured it, condemned it.

Jacob's Ladder

THE PATRIARCH JACOB DROVE an amazing life. Escaping his brother, Esau (whom he had conned out of his legacy), Jacob spent a night in the wilds, utilizing a stone for a cushion. He had a dream of a stairway to paradise, with blessed angels going up and down it. (Older interpretations utilize "Ladder" rather than "stairway.")

Over the stairway God Himself talked and renewed His covenant with Jacob's relatives. Jacob awoke and concluded, "Without a doubt the LORD is in this place...This is none other than the house of God, and this is the door of paradise!" (Gen. 28:16,17). Jacob named the spot Bethel ("place of God").

Wrestling God (Or An Angel)

JACOB, GRANDSON OF ABRAHAM, had a beautiful life, and Genesis 32 tells how he truly wrestled God, or God's holy messenger. On the lam from his irate brother, Esau, Jacob met a man who grappled with him till sunrise. The man tore Jacob's hip out of its attachment, at that point requested to go; yet Jacob answered, "I won't let You go except if You bless me!" (Genesis 32:26). The man (or heavenly attendant) revealed to Jacob that from that point on his name would be Israel, signifying "battles with God," since Jacob had "battled with God and with men, and (had) won" (Gen. 32:28). The man (or blessed angel) would not reveal to Jacob his very own name, and Jacob - now renamed Israel - reasoned that he had seen God face-to-face.

The Burning Bush

EXODUS 3 RECOUNTS THE celebrated story of Moses experiencing the consuming hedge in the wild: "And the Angel of the LORD appeared to him in a fire of flame from the middle of a shrub. So he looked, and see, the shrubbery consumed with flame, yet the hedge was not expended" (Exod. 3:2). Be that as it may, later on in the story there is no notice of the holy angel of the Lord, only the Lord Himself. So who was there – the Lord or he holy angel? This is one of a few places in the Bible where the appropriate response is by all accounts "both." Clearly the heavenly angel of the Lord was one that the author took to be God Himself.

The Angel At The Red Sea

THE TEN COMMANDMENTS OF the Bible delineates so strikingly, the Israelite slaves' exit from abusive Egypt was sensational. Their departure appears to be unlikely to the point that it tends to be clarified just as perfect intercession.

Just before the popular separating of the Red Sea, Exodus records that "the Angel of God, who went before the camp of Israel, moved and went behind them; and the mainstay of cloud went from before them and remained behind them. So it separated the camp of the Egyptians and the camp of Israel.

Dr. John Thomas Wylie

In this way it was a cloud and darkness to the one, and it gave light by night to the next, with the goal that the one didn't draw close to the next such night" (Exod. 14:19,20). In this way God's holy angel filled in as a sort of support until the point when God separated the Red Sea for the Israelites to go through securely.

The Angel On Sinai

THE BOOK OF EXODUS reveals to us that God Himself gave the Law straightforwardly to Moses on Mount Sinai. In the book of Acts, the saint Stephen had it to some degree in an unexpected way, alluding to the holy angel who addressed Moses on Sinai (Exod. 7:38). An inconsistency? Not really. Enter occasions in the Bible are frequently revealed in various ways: A man meets with God Himself in one adaptation of a story, with the Lord's holy angel in another. In any case, the primary thought is that God' power came through in the gathering.

The Israelites' Angel

EXODUS 23 CONTAINS A few promises - and threats - to Israel, God's people. God promised that He would send a blessed angel "to keep you in the path and to carry you into the place which I have prepared. Be careful with him and comply with His voice; don't incite Him, for He won't acquit your transgressions; for My name is Him" (Exod. 23:20, 21).

In these verses God isn't talking around a blessed angel that anybody can see or hear, but instead an undetectable guide. A few Christians later connected these words to Christ, saying that He will guide God's people to the place prepared for them-not to Canaan, but rather to paradise.

Christ In The Old Testament

THE EARLY CHRISTIANS, SINCE the greater part of them were Jews, perused and cherished the Old Testament. Since they trusted that Jesus Christ was the Messiah who the prophets had anticipated, they scanned the Old Testament for anything that may give off an impression of being a prescience of the Christ. Some went so far as to state that the "holy angel of the Lord" made reference to ordinarily in the Old Testament was Christ Himself, showing up before He was really conceived as a human child in Bethlehem.

The Passover

A DAY JEWS CELEBRATE remembering God's "ignoring: the Hebrews' homes as He caused the demise of the firstborn of the Egyptians. Moses advised the general population to stamp their homes with blood, and the holy messenger of death "ignored" them (Ex. 12:23). This last of the ten torment on the Egyptians had the coveted impact: Pharaoh discharged the Hebrew slaves. Reviewing the motion picture "The Ten Commandments," the passing blessed messenger was delineated as a kind of vile, deadly haze moving over the scene.

Balaam's donkey

CAN A DONKEY TALK? The prophet Balaam had such a creature, at any rate on one event. As the Israelites ventured from Egypt to their home in Canaan, they went through the antagonistic place where there is Moab. The Moabite king sent his prophet Balaam to revile Israel. As Balaam rode toward the Israelites his donkey saw a heavenly angel with an drawn sword the road.

The donkey veered off, and Balaam beat her, not seeing the blessed angel himself. The poor at long last set down, and Balaam beat her once more. This time she spoke: "What have I done to you, that you have struck me these three times?" (Num. 22:28). God opened Balaam's eyes, and he saw the blessed angel and fell facedown. He normally, changed his designs and as opposed to reviling the Israelites, he forecasted that they would be an incredible country, blessed by God (Num. 22:28-32).

Joshua Fit De Battle Of Jericho

THE OLD SPIRITUAL DEPENDS on Joshua 5:13-6:27. Joshua, pioneer of the Israelites after Moses died, was told by a holy angel (the commander of the Lord's armed force) how to catch the unequivocally fortified city of Jericho. Rather than attacking, the Israelites were to walk around the city for six days, carrying the ark of the covenant. On the seventh day, priests were to blow trumpets and the general population were to shout. When they did this, the city walls fell (as the tune says, "and de dividers come tumblin' down"), and the Israelites captured the city.

The "Commander of the LORD'S Army" needed to advise Joshua to remove his shoes, for he was standing on holy ground. This is actually what the Lord told Moses to do when talking from the consuming bush, so we have motivation to surmise that the "Commander" was simply the Lord.

The Angel Of Bochim

THE HEBREW WORD BOCHIM signifies "weeping," and it was at Bochim that the general population of Israel had great purpose to sob. Judges 2 talks about the heavenly angel of the Lord meeting with the general population there, advising them that they had been unfaithful to the Lord. Thus, the barbarian (heathen), clans around them "will be thorns in your side, and their gods will be a snare to you" (2:3). Becoming aware of this, the general population broke into weeping. As the book of Judges clarifies, the heavenly angel's prediction worked out.

Gideon's Angel

JUDGES 6 STARTS THE story of the military pioneer Gideon. While sifting wheat, Gideon was welcomed by a blessed angel with the words "The Lord is with you, you powerful man of valor!" (6:12)). Gideon was doubtful and expressed that the Lord was not with him, nor his country, for the Lord had given the Midianites a chance to persecute them. (The Midianites - the voracious "camel racers" of the Old Testament - were a consistent headache for Israel). In any case, the blessed angel demanded that Gideon would be the one to convey Israel from the Midianites.

As regularly occurs in the Old Testament, this puzzling guest is distinguished as "the holy angel of the Lord" however then is designated "the Lord" a couple of verses later. Were the creators befuddled? No. The primary point was that the errand person (angel) was speaking the word of God. At any rate, Gideon needed a sign that the guest was really divine.

He set some uncooked meat and bread on a stone, and the heavenly angel set them ablaze with the end of his staff. At that point the holy angel vanished. Gideon was awestruck: "Too bad, O Lord GOD! For I have seen the Angel of the LORD face to face" (Judges 6:11-22).

Samson's Birth

THE HEBREW STRONGMAN IS one of the all the more intriguing Bible characters, possibly on the grounds that his story includes savagery, desire, disloyalty, and vengeance. His story is told in Judges 13-16. Samson was one of Israel's "judges" - not a judge in the advanced sense, but rather more like a deliverer or military pioneer.

Israel was tormented continually by the agnostic Philistines. Samson was destined to a woman who had for quite some time been desolate (barren), and a holy angel advised his folks to dedicate the child to God.

The Post-Census Plague

KING DAVID DIRECTED A registration (census) of Israel, something that maddened the Lord incredibly. The prophet Gad disclosed to David that awesome discipline was en route, and it came as a plague that murdered seventy thousand individuals. The plague was evidently crafted by the Lord's blessed angel.

Seeing all the devastation (destruction), the Lord halted the heavenly angel. "At that point David addressed the LORD when he saw the blessed angel who was striking the general population: (II Sam. 24:10-17).

As so regularly occurs in the Bible, we have no clue what the holy angel looked like or how David could establish that he was a heavenly angel. In any case, David repented of his indiscretion and assembled a sacred place (altar) to the Lord, and the plague was finished.

The Heavenly Host

THE KING JAMES VERSION of the Bible uses have in an old sense, signifying "army" or "multitude." In the KJV, have more often than not alludes to an exacting human armed force, however several times it particularly alludes to "the hosts of heaven" or "heavenly host," which are unmistakably heavenly beings.

These could be holy angels, however "host of heaven" can likewise speak to the stars and planets. The prophet Micaiah asserted that he "saw the LORD sitting on His throne, and all the host of heaven standing by, on His right hand and to His left" (I Kings 22:19). The phrase "the LORD of hosts" happens commonly in the Bible, alluding to God's power and majesty.

Likely the most well known mention of the heavenly host happens in the account of the blessed angels and the shepherds of Bethlehem: "And all of a sudden there was with the holy angel a multitude of the heavenly host praising God and saying: "Glory to God in the highest, and on earth peace, good will toward men!" (Luke 2:13-14).

Elijah's Angel

ISRAEL'S PROPHETS CONTINUALLY PREACHED against their people's idol worship. The Canaanite fertility god Baal was one of numerous false gods the Israelites worshiped. The incredible prophet Elijah tested 450 prophets of Baal to a confrontation on Mount Carmel (I Kings 18). There the excited Baal prophets had no accomplishment in calling down Baal to eat up the animals they sacrificed, however Elijah's God sent down fire (potentially lightning to consume the sacrifice. When the general population saw that God was the true God, "they fell on their faces; and they stated, "The LORD, HE is God!" (I Kings 18:39).

The occurrence made Queen Jezebel, an infamous baal worshiper, resolved to murder Elijah. So straight from his triumph over Baal's prophets, he fled to the desert, where God helped him. "As he lay and rested under a floor brush tree, all of a sudden a heavenly angel touched him, and said to him, 'Arise and eat.' Then he looked, and there by his head was a cake heated on coals, and a container of water" (I Kings 19:5-6).

Elijah And Beelzebub

BLESSED ANGELS SHOWED UP in beautiful existence of the prophet Elijah. In II Kings 1 is the story of how Israel's king Ahaziah, injured from a fall, sent envoys to the Philistine god

Beelzebub. As it were, a man dreading passing solicited the workers from a false god whether he would live or die.

"In any case, the heavenly angel of the LORD said to Elijah the Tishbite, 'Arise, go up to meet the messengers of the king" (v. 3). The holy angel trained Elijah to reprimand the king for disregarding Israel's own God and inquisitive of an agnostic icon. (This was what might as well be called fiddling with the occult). The message deteriorated: The king would die from his wounds. It happened as predicted.

The Destruction Of Sennacherib

THE RIGHTEOUS KING HEZEKIAH's reign is depicted in II Kings 18-20. He defied the realm of Assyria, which prompted Jerusalem's being debilitated by the relentless King Sennacherib. The prophet Isaiah revealed to Hezekiah that God would carry them from the fierce Assyrians. The holy angel of the Lord struck down 185,000 Assyrian soldiers and Sennacherib returned home-to be killed by his own sons.

The Assembled sons Of God

THE BOOK OF JOB opens with a depiction of the noble man Job, trailed by a kind of "court scene:" "Now there was a day when the sons of God came to present themselves before the LORD, and Satan (fallen angel) likewise came among them" (1:6). In spite of the fact that they are not alluded to as heavenly angels, we can just accept that that is the thing that these "sons of God" are.

Charging The Angels With Error

WOULD ANGELS BE ABLE to commit errors? In the book of Job, Job's three companions attempt to disclose to him why such a significant number of cataclysms have happened to him. Eliphaz, one of the three companions, inquire as to whether he truly thought himself so righteous: "If He (God) puts no trust in His servants (angels), if He accuses His heavenly angels of mistake, the amount increasingly the individuals who abide in places of mud" (4:18-19).

Put another way, if God's very own heavenly chaperons (angels) can fail (and Eliphaz infers that they can), at that point without a doubt not any more human is above committing an error from time to time.

The Morning Stars Sang

IN THE ANCIENT WORLD, the faraway stars and planets appeared to be puzzling even celestial. In this manner, most old people groups fell into the blunder of revering the magnificent bodies. Israel's prophets continually railed against this (and the love of anything aside from the genuine God).

The Hebrews would not acknowledge the magnificent bodies as divine beings, yet the Bible clues that they trusted the stars were holy angels. Consider Job 38, where the Lord Himself defies Job and questions him: "Where were you when I established the frameworks of the earth?...When the morning stars sang together, and all the sons of God shouted for joy?" (38:4, 7). Unmistakably the "morning stars" and the "sons of God" allude to holy angels.

"A Little Lower Than The Angels"

PSALM 8 IS A melody of praise to God, respecting the wonders of creation. Contrasted and this limitlessness, where does man fit in?

"When I think about Your heavens, crafted by Your fingers, the moon and the stars, which You have ordained, what is man that You are aware of him, and the son of man that You visit him?

For You have made him a little lower than the heavenly angels, and You have delegated him with glory and honor" (Psalm 8:3-5). We have the expression "holy messengers" in our English interpretation, yet the real Hebrew word is elohim, which can be deciphered as "gods" or "heavenly beings." But "angels" is a reasonable interpretation, since the psalm is clearly alluding to God's "heavenly court."

God's Transportation

AS INDICATED BY PSALM 18, God can utilize a holy angel as a method of transportation: "He rode upon a cherub, and flew; He flew upon the wings of the wind" (v. 10). This sort of cherub isn't the charming, thick infant heavenly angel the vast majority consider, yet a remarkable, winged creature, for example, the two on the highest point of the ark of the covenant (cherubim).

Dr. John Thomas Wylie

Angel Security

PSALM 34 IS A beautiful proclamation of trust in perfect security. Consider verse 7: "The heavenly angel of the LORD encamps all around the individuals who fear Him, and delivers them." The word "encamps" recommends one holy angel as well all in all army of blessed angels, hovering to secure the individual.

The general population of Israel had seen over and over the saving activities of God and His holy angels, so it is suitable that this tune of trust alludes to the blessed angels and their protective work.

Angels In Pursuit

PSALM 35 IS THE call of a persecuted man petitioning God for deliverance and retribution on his persecutors. "Let those be put to shame and brought to dishonor who seek after my life... Let them resemble debris before the wind, and let the blessed angel of the LORD pursue them.

Give their direction a chance to be dim and dangerous, and let the blessed angel of the LORD seek after them" (vv. 4-6). While this strikes a few perusers as wrathful (even unchristian) we need to peruse it for what it is: the ardent cry of one being mistreated. The man isn't looking for his own retaliation, however is asking God and His heavenly angels to bring it about.

Chariots Of God

AN APPROPRIATE TITLE FOR Psalm 68 may be "God Rules!" It is a melody of triumph, just as God were a heavenly winner marching in glory to Jerusalem. "The chariots of God are twenty-thousand, even a huge number of holy angels" (Psalm 68:17).

Does this imply God truly rides holy angels as a man would ride in a chariot? No! It is essentially a poetic method for saying that God, the Ruler of the universe, is joined by a large number of holy angels, a reality specified more than once in the Bible.

Evil Angels In Egypt

THE LONG PSALM 78 is a sort of speedy audit of Israel's history, the great and the awful. Several verses allude to the maladies sent upon Egypt. Note verse 49: "He cast on them the furiousness of His anger, wrath, indignation, and trouble, by sending holy angels of destruction," a few interpretations have "evil angels.")

This verse brings to mind the vile, evil fog in the film, "The Ten Commandments." Instead of a real angel with wings, the blessed messenger of death (which slaughters all the firstborn of the Egyptians) is portrayed as a black fog creeping over the land.

"They Shall Bear You Up"

A STANDOUT AMONGST THE most soothing of the "protection" hymns is Psalm 91, with its guarantees of awesome guide. Consider this area: "He will give His holy angels charge over you, to keep you in the entirety of your ways. In their grasp, they will bear you up, for fear that you dash your foot against a stone" (vv.1`1,12).

Recognizable? These words were cited by Satan (evil angel) when he tempted Jesus to divert Himself from the apex of the temple (Matt. 4:6). Presumably Jesus knew this wonderful hymn well, yet He could see that Satan was bending the words for his very own motivations. Jesus countered with His very own citation from Scripture: "You will not tempt the LORD your God" (Deut. 6:16).

Angelic Sing-Along

PRAISE IS A KEY subject of a large number of the psalms, and unquestionably Psalm 103 is a standout amongst the most sincere outpourings of praise anyplace in the Bible. David, its creator, starts by lauding God with his deepest being, however toward the end he enrolls the guide of different voices:

"Bless the LORD, you His heavenly angels, who exceed expectations in strength, who do His word, heeding the voice of His word. Bless the LORD, all you His hosts, you ministers of His, who do His pleasure" (vv.20,21).

Genesis Set To Music

ONE BIBLE DISCOURSE GIVES this name to Psalm 104, a generous melody of acclaim for God's creation. Normally, holy angels consider along with the melody: "He lays the light emissions upper chambers in the waters, who makes the mists His chariot, who strolls of the breeze, who makes His holy angels spirits, His priests a fire of flame" (vv. 3,4). "Fire of flame" here may just mean lightning. It seems as though God is riding upon tempest mists, encompassed by heavenly angels as winds and lightning.

Isaiah's Vision

THE PROPHET ISAIAH IN Isaiah 6, recorded his "commissioning" by God, which happened in a vision in which seraphs (holy angels) were singing praise to God. Isaiah was awestruck to the point that he shouted out, "Woe is me!" Lamenting that he was a debased man living among polluted individuals.

One of the seraphs took a live coal from the altar, touched Isaiah's mouth, and announced him purged (purified). At that point God asked, "Whom will I send?" Isaiah answered, "Here am I! send me."

Seraphim

LIKE THE CHERUBIM THE seraphim were a kind of heavenly angel. (Seraphim is plural-one seraph, two seraphim). Their name implies, so far as we probably am aware, "consuming ones"

Dr. John Thomas Wylie

or "burning ones." They are specified in Isaiah's vision in the temple, and they established a significant connection: "Every one had six wings: and two he secured his face, with two he secured his feet, and with two he flew" (Isa. 6:2). This is the only mention of seraphim in the Bible.

Jewish fables holds that the seraphim were the most astounding request among the holy angels. They were not couriers, as most other heavenly angels, but rather were attendants to God, regularly praising His power and holiness.

In art, seraphim are usually appeared in red (since they are the "burning ones"), regularly conveying the flabellum, a blazing sword engraved with "Holy, holy, holy" the words they spoke in Isaiah's vision.

Cherubim

THE EXPRESSION "SERAPHS" MORE often than not alludes to the charming, chubby heavenly attendants found on many a Christmas cards. In any case, in the Bible they are wonderful, relatively startling creatures. The prophet Ezekiel had an abnormal vision of the cherubim (that is plural one angel, two cherubim): "Their entire body, with their back, their hands, their wings, and the wheels that the four had, were brimming with eyes all around...Each one had four faces: the main face was the essence of a seraph, the second face the substance of a man, the third essence of a lion, and the fourth the essence of a eagle" (Ezek. 10:12, 14).

Considerably prior, cherubim had filled in as sentries, display flaming swords to keep Adam and Eve out once they were expelled from Eden (Gen. 3:24).

The most generally observed cherubim-or, in any event, figures of them - were the two on the cover of he ark of the covenant. The ark is depicted in detail in Exodus 25, including the two winged figures who confront one another, their wings touching.

Israel was restricted from making pictures of God Himself, yet clearly they thought of the space between the cherubim as where God was present: The expression "LORD Almighty, enthroned between the cherubim" happens many times in the Bible.

"The Angel Of His Presence"

ISAIAH 63 PERUSES LIKE a hymn, with its affectionate recognitions of God's guide in the past to the Israelites: "In the entirety of their afflictions He was afflicteded, and the Angel of His presence saved them" (v. 9). We don't know whether this holy angel was a specific blessed messenger, or if this is only a poetic method for saying, "His presence saved them."

Ezekiel's Living Creatures

THE BOOK OF THE prophet Ezekiel opens with a blast, the prophet's strange vision of four unearthly creatures. Amidst an inauspicious whirlwind were "four living creatures." They were human fit as a fiddle, yet every one had four wings, and their feet resembled calves' feet. They shimmered like polished bronze. Each had four faces: a lion, a man, a ox, and a eagle.

They moved, and they gave the impression of fire and lightning. More amazing than the creatures was simply the glory of the Lord above them.

This shocking vision made Ezekiel to fall upon his face, whereupon the Lord commissioned him as a prophet to the general population of Israel.

We learn in Ezekiel 10 that these "living creatures" are cherubim, the guardians of the Lord's throne. Since this vision occurred in Babylon, where Ezekiel was in a state of banishment, one message is by all accounts that the Lord's throne of is anyplace He wishes it to be, not really fixing to an area in Israel.

Angel Eyes

Ezekiel 10 records the prophet's sensational experience with the cherubim (a kind of angel). In contrast to most different heavenly angels in the Bible, these cherubim were absolutely unearthly in appearance: "The entire body, and their backs, and their hands, and their wings, and the wheels, were brimming with eyes circuitous: (v. 12).

This depiction is the reason a few specialists have depicted holy angels with eyes on their wings. (The eyes show that the blessed angels see everything). A few blessed angels have even been depicted with wings that resemble peacock plumes, presumably in light of the fact that the circlets at the closures of peacock quills look much like eyes.

A Friend In The Furnace

THERE IS SOMETHING EXTRAORDINARY and melodic about the names of the prophet Daniel's three companions (friends): Shadrach, Meshach, and Abed-Nego. Daniel 3 recounts the story of how devilish King Nebuchadnezzar of Babylon had the three companions tossed into a fiery furnace. A short time later, the king discovered that not exclusively were the three men surviving the furnace, however there were "four men free, walking amidst the fire; and they were not harmed, and the type of the fourth was like the Son of God" (v. 25).

Nebuchadnezzar was impressed to the point that he stated, "Blessed be the God of Shadraach, Meshach, and Abed-Nego, who sent His Angel and delivered His servants" (v. 28).

Angel In The Lion's Den

DANIEL THE HEBREW PROPHET confronted the test of living under outside rulers who worshiped other gods. Daniel 6 recounts the commonplace story of how the Persian king Darius had Daniel tossed into a den of lions for petitioning his own God. The following morning, much incredibly, Daniel was perfectly healthy. He told the lord, "My God sent His heavenly angel and close the lion's mouths" (6:22).

Watchers And Holy Ones

HOLY ANGELS ASSUME A noticeable job in the book of Daniel. In Daniel 4, the prophet relates, "I found in the visions of my head while on my bed, and there was a watcher, a holy one, descending from paradise" (v. 13). We can likely accept that this watcher and holy one was a holy angel.

Jewish legend relates that heavenly angels never rested. Jewish legend likewise has it that the watchers were the "sons of God" made reference to in Genesis 6, who lived together with human women and brought forth a race of giants.

Daniel's Heavenly Interpreter

THE BOOK OF DANIEL, similar to the book of Revelation in the New Testament, contains visions that are difficult to translate. Daniel had a dream of four abnormal brutes leaving the sea. The holy angel Gabriel was the brilliant mediator who disclosed the visions to Daniel.

The blessed angel told Daniel, "Understand, son of man, that the vision alludes to the time of the end...I am making known to you what will occur in the last time of the indignation" (Dan. 8:17,19).

The Man Clothed In Linen

NOT ALL HOLY ANGELS in the Bible are related to the word "angel." Both Ezekiel and Daniel notice "a man dressed in linen," and in the settings plainly it was a heavenly angel being alluded to.

In Ezekiel 9 and 10, the man dressed in material (linen) has an author's inkwell next to him, so unmistakably this holy angel is a sort of eminent recorder)(a angelic scribe). Jewish convention says it was the heavenly angel Michael or Enoch the patriarch.

Zechariah's Angels

EXCEPTIONAL AMONG EVERY ONE of the books of the prophets in the Old Testament, Zechariah records a few experiences with blessed angels. Nearly toward the start of his book, he talks about a "man" (plainly this is a blessed angel) riding a red horse, with three different horses behind him. The prophet discovers that the horses and riders have been going forward and backward all through the earth (1:7-11).

Later in the book, a blessed angel translates different images to the prophet, including a lampstand, a flying scroll, and a woman in a basket. In chapter 6, the prophet sees horses and chariots of four distinct colors, and the blessed angel clarifies that they are "four spirits of paradise, who go out from their station before the Lord of all the earth" (v. 5).

Stork Angels

THE BOOK OF THE prophet Zechariah makes reference to holy angels a few times, principally in the job of translating visions. (A blessed angel assumed a similar job for the prophet Daniel). However, Zechariah additionally makes reference to something different that sounds faintly heavenly: "At that point I raised my eyes and looked, and there were two women, accompanying the wind in their wings; for they had wings like the wings of a stork" (5:9).

Malakh

THE HEBREW WORD UTILIZED "angel" in the Old Testament is "malakh," signifying "dispatcher or messenger," not really a powerful one. We need to decide from the setting that the specific "malakh" is without a doubt a heavenly angel, not a customary human courier.

By chance, the prophet Malachi, whose book closes the Old Testament, bears a name that interprets as "my delegate or my messenger." Bible researchers aren't sure in the event that he was named Malachi or if the book is kind of mysterious as though it were titled "A Prophecy by God's Messenger."

Chapter

TWO

The Life Of Jesus

Logos And Angel Of The Lord

JOHN'S GOSPEL STARTS WITH "In the beginning was the Word, and the Word was with God, and the Word was God." As he continues further, clearly he recognizes this Word with Christ. The early Christians by and large trusted that Christ had somehow existed from the earliest starting point. He was the pre-existing Word (which interprets the Greek word "logos").

Some early Christians noticed the occasions in the Old Testament that the expression "angel of the Lord" shows up and chose that the holy angel of the Lord may be the "Logos" showing up before He turned into the God-man Jesus Christ. At the end of the day, the Logos had been putting in appearances among individuals for a few centuries.

John The Baptist

JOHN WAS THE BROTHER and forerunner of Jesus Christ and one of the Bible's most fascinating characters. John's introduction to the world was, similar to Jesus', declared by the blessed angel Gabriel, and he was destined to the elderly couple Zechariah and Elizabeth. Gabriel foretold that the child would act "in the spirit and power of Elijah...to make ready people prepared for the Lord" (Luke 1:17).

Joseph, The Angel, And Dreams

THE FIRST MENTION OF a blessed angel in the four Gospels happens regarding the introduction of Jesus. Mary, Joseph's fiancee, was pregnant through the work of the Holy Spirit. Looked with a troublesome circumstance, Joseph was visited in a dream by a holy angel, who let him know, "Joseph, son of David, don't be hesitant to take to you Mary your wife, for that which is conceived in her is of the Holy Spirit.

What's more, she will deliver a Son, and you will call His name JESUS, for He will save His people from their sins" (Matt. 1:20,21). Joseph paid attention to the blessed angel's words, wedded Mary, and named the child Jesus.

After the introduction of Jesus and the visit of the wise men from the East, Joseph got another visit from the heavenly angel, and in light of current circumstances: Wicked king Herod had heard the gossip that a "King of the Jews" had been conceived, and he wanted to make a grisly bloody move.

The holy angel told Joseph, "Arise, take the young child and His mother, escape to Egypt, and remain there until the point when I bring you word; for Herod will look for the youthful Child to demolish Him" (Matt. 2:13).

Herod (Known to history as "Herod the Great," despite the fact that everybody concurs he was completely terrible) requested all the male children in Bethlehem butchered, however at this point Jesus was securely in Egypt. The heavenly angel visited Joseph again and let him know it was safe to return home (vv. 13-23).

Jesus The Ladder

THE EARLY CHRISTIANS THOUGHT of Jesus as the perfect Mediator between corrupt man and the blessed God. In John's gospel, Jesus expressed these puzzling words: "You will see paradise open, and the blessed angels of God ascending and descending upon the Son of Man" (1:51). Plainly Jesus had as a main priority the dream of Jacob in Genesis 28, in which he saw a ladder (or stairway) to paradise, with heavenly angels going all over upon it. The blessed angels going back and forth spoke to God's correspondence with man, which Jesus shows presently happens through Him.

The Angel Of The Pool

JOHN'S GOSPEL MAKES REFERENCE to a pool in Jerusalem, a pool with inexplicable forces of recuperating (healing). "A heavenly angel) went down at a specific time into the pool and stirred up or troubled the water; at that point whoever ventured in first, after the troubling of the water, was made well of whatever sickness he had" (t:4). The story proceeds with Jesus' recuperating a poor man who had attempted futile to get to the pool's mending water yet was never the first in.

An old Christian legend has it that it was the blessed angel Raphael who troubled the waters (since the name Raphael signifies "God heals").

The Angel In The Garden

THE GOSPELS DISCLOSE TO us that Jesus, being completely human, endured misery before His capture, realizing that He would be crucified. Luke's gospel records that in the garden on the Mount of Olives He petitioned God, "Father if it is Your will, remove this cup from Me; all things considered not My will, but Yours, be done.' Then a holy angel appeared to Him from Heaven, fortifying Him" (Luke 22:42, 43).

A few perusers ask why the Son of God would need such guide, however we have to recollect that Jesus was completely human and could profit by heavenly help similarly as any human would. In numerous works of art of Jesus' misery in the garden, a holy angel is appeared.

Twelve Legions

JESUS' BETRAYAL BY JUDAS and His capture in the Garden of Gethsemane made one of His followers lash out in savagery. Jesus quickly let him know, "Put your sword in its place, for all who take the sword will die by the sword. Or on the other hand do you believe that I can't presently go to My Father, and He will give Me in excess of twelve armies of holy angels?" (Matt. 26:52,53)' It is evident that Jesus was aware of the power of God to follow up for His sake, yet He realized that the way for suffering and dying on the cross was the only way.

The Angel And The Stone

To the inquiry "How did Jesus escape His tomb?" the Gospels give an answer: "Observe, there was an incredible seismic tremor (earthquake); for a blessed angel of the Lord plummeted from paradise, and returned and rolled the stone from the entryway, and sat on it. His face resembled lightning, and his garments as white as snow.

What's more, the watchmen shook inspired by a paranoid fear of him, and ended up like dead men" (Matt. 28:2-4). To the committed women who had gone to the tomb, the holy angel said that Jesus was not there, for He had risen (28:5,6). It appears to be proper, since there were heavenly angels associated with Jesus' origination and birth, that a holy angel would be at the scene of the Resurrection.

The Angels In The Tomb

Every one of the Gospels record holy angels regarding Jesus' empty tomb. John's gospel relates that Mary Magdalene, the committed follower of Jesus, came right off the bat Easter morning to the tomb and thought that it was unfilled. "Also, she saw two heavenly angels in white sitting, one at the head and the other at the feet, where the body of Jesus had lain" (20:12).

The Ignorance Of Angels

AT THE POINT WHEN is the end of time? At the point when will Jesus come back to earth? Individuals have been hypothesizing about this for a considerable length of time, and nobody has taken care of business yet. In addition to the fact that people are oblivious of the time, Jesus stated, are the blessed angels: "Of that day and hour nobody knows, not by any means the holy angels of paradise, but My Father only" (Matt. 24:36).

Chapter
THREE

Angels And The Apostles

The Apostles' Liberator

ACTS 5 RELATES THAT the Jewish authorities slapped the missionaries in jail. They weren't there long, for "during the night a heavenly angel of the Lord opened the jail entryways and brought them out, and stated, 'Go, remain in the temple and address the general population every one of the expressions of this life.' And when they heard that, they entered the temple at a young hour early in the day and taught." (vv. 19,20).

The jail monitors revealed, "We found the jail close safely, and the watchmen (guards) remaining outside before the entryways; however when we opened them, we found nobody inside!" (v. 23).

Philip's Angel

THE BOOK OF ACTS reveals to us much about Philip, one of the seven "deacons" who helped the Christians in Jerusalem. He is generally called "Philip the evangelist" since Acts records his conveying the gospel to far-flung regions. He was pushed to do as such by a superb emissary: A holy angel instructed him to go toward a desert street, where he met an authority of the queen of the Ethiopians.

Evidently this authority was a "God-fearer," a non-Jew who was pulled in to the Jewish religion. At the point when Philip discovered him, he was in his chariot. Philip disclosed the gospel to him and instantly absolved him. Clearly the experience was great, for the Ethiopian "went on his way rejoicing" (Acts 8:26-39). Along these lines, in a brief span after Jesus' resurrection, the gospel had effectively moved as far as to the kingdom of Ethiopia.

Cornelius And Peter

A STANDOUT AMONGST THE most engaging characters in the New Testament is Cornelius, a Roman centurion. Acts 10 depicts him as "one who dreaded God," which implied he practiced a Jewish spirituality, including supplication and supporting poor people. Acts 10 relates his being visited by a blessed angel, who revealed to him that his graciousness and benevolent acts had not gone unnoticed by God. The blessed angel connected him with the missionary Peter. After his gathering with Peter, he became a Christian, the first Roman believer to the faith of Christianity.

Angels, Not Evangelists

BLESSED ANGELS IN THE Bible do numerous things to benefit people, including declaring the introduction of the Savior (Luke 2). In any case, there is one unmistakable action that holy angels don't do: preach the gospel. One model: Acts 10 lets us know of the honest Roman officer Cornelius, who was advised by a heavenly angel to send for the witness Peter, the man who might preach him the gospel.

For what reason didn't simply the holy angel present the gospel? This never occurs in the Bible, nor anyplace in Christian history. The gospel is the uplifting news of sinners being saved from their sins something heavenly angels can't experience themselves. Only a saved sinner can preach the gospel to sinners.

Peter And The Angel

As Jesus anticipated, His witnesses were oppressed, detained, and even executed. Peter was tossed into jail by Herod and bound in chains with a soldier on each side. Peter was sleeping but stirred (awakened) to a glowing heavenly angel, who made Peter's chains tumble off.

Peter followed him out and went to a home where some kindred Christians were petitioning God for him. At the point when Peter knocked, the servant young girl was crazy at seeing him set free. Peter's phenomenal deliverance had a heartbreaking ramification for his gatekeepers: Herod had them executed (Acts 12).

The Death Of Herod

Acts 12 records the persecution of Christians by the savage, violent ruler Herod. He killed the apostle James and had Peter detained for a period. Be that as it may, a desperate destiny anticipated Herod himself. Showing up in his regal robes and giving an articulate discourse before a group, Herod established such a connection, to the point that the general population hollered, "The voice of a divine being (god) and not of a man!"

Maybe Herod's inner self had swelled too enormous; "At that point instantly a heavenly angel of the Lord struck him, since he didn't offer glory to God. And he was eaten by worms and died" (Acts 12:23).

Paul's Shipwreck

PAUL THE MISSIONARY HAD an existence with many intriguing scratches and escapes, and Acts 27 recounts an emotional tempest and wreck. The tempest seethed for a considerable length of time, and nearly everything was tossed over the edge. The group was going to lose hope, yet Paul (on his approach to preliminary in Rome) declared that a holy angel had guaranteed him that he would reach Rome, and however the ship would be lost, nobody would pass on.

The ship steered into the rocks on Malta, and the officers on board intended to execute the detainees, dreading they would endeavor to get away. Be that as it may, a Roman centurion who clearly liked Paul shielded the warriors from executing anybody.

A Spectacle Before The Angels

ARE BLESSED ANGELS TRULY "watchin' over me," as the old camp melody says? Indeed. Paul composed that "we have been made a scene to the world, both to blessed angels and to men" (I Cor. 4:9). Inside Paul's very own lifetime, a portion of the scenes appeared as persecution in the enormous Roman arenas, where Christians were tormented and ruthlessly killed for the delight of the cold-hearted gatherings of people.

The holy angels were viewing. So while Christians who endured in the Roman scenes may hear chuckling and scoffs from their crowds, they knew that God and His heavenly angels were a more vital audience.

Angels Or Spirit?

GENERALLY, HOLY ANGELS ARE imperceptible to man, just like the Holy Spirit. A few people confound the two, trusting that the Spirit is a holy angel. The Bible is certain that heavenly angels are "ministering spirits" (Heb. 1:14), but additionally evident that blessed angels are not to be worshiped (Col. 2:18).

Blessed angels are creatures, not the Creator, and only the Creator is to be worshiped (Rom. 1:24, 25). The Spirit is simply the triune God, convicting men for transgression (sin) and judgment (John 16:8), uncovering and deciphering Christ to men, and never uncovering Himself in human form, as blessed angels in some cases do.

The Spirit can be in excess of one place at any given moment, however a holy angel can't. The Spirit is all-present, all-knowing, and all-powerful. While blessed angel's capacities far surpass our own, they don't have the abilities of the Spirit.

Judging The Angels

PAUL THE APOSTLE EXPRESSED in I Corinthians, "Do you not realize that the holy people will pass judgment on the world?... Do you not realize that we will pass judgment on blessed angels?" (6:2,3). This makes numerous perusers stop. In what manner can simple mortals ever be placed in the situation of making a decision about the radiant heavenly angels?

A few places in the New Testament demonstrate that a portion of the blessed angels will be judged (Matt. 25:41; II Peter 2:4; Jude 6). There is unquestionably no reason behind why the resurrected believers, ruling with Christ, would not take an interest in the judging decision of blessed angels who had become out of line.

Armor Of Angels

THE MESSENGER PAUL TALKED in Romans 13:12 of the "armor of light" and in II Corinthians 6:7 of the "armor of righteousness" that Christians should wear. Heavenly angels have regularly been depicted in workmanship as wearing armor also.

This appears to be proper, since convention has it that they are the "hosts" (armies) of the Lord. The lead celestial host Michael, whom the Bible notices as making war on Satan, is quite often imagined in armor or some likeness thereof.

Company Of Angels

FOR THE JEWS, MOUNT Sinai was an uncommon place, where God gave His heavenly Law to Moses. The Letter to the Hebrews asserts that there is presently a holier place than Sinai: "the city of the living God, the radiant Jerusalem" with its "endless organization of blessed angels," the place of "the firstborn who are enlisted in paradise" and "the spirits of just men made perfect" (12:22,23).

Curious Angels

AS PER I PETER, the proclaiming of the Christian good news of salvation is such a magnificent thing, that even the blessed angels want to investigate it (1:12).

The Court Scene

JESUS IN PARADISE IS (allegorically) at the right hand of God. In I Peter, we discover that Christ "is at the right hand of God, blessed angels and authorities and powers having been made subject to Him." Peter was envisioning a heavenly court, with the heavenly angels, authorities, and powers (three unique classifications of holy angels) subject to their Ruler, Christ.

Nothing Will Separate Us

THE APOSTLE PAUL WAS sure that once a heathen was redeemed by Christ, nothing at all could isolate him from God. "I am convinced that neither death nor life, nor holy angels nor principalities nor powers, nor things present nor things to come, nor height nor depth, nor any other made thing, will have the capacity to separate us from the love of God which is in Christ Jesus our Lord" (Rom. 8:38,39).

This is one of a couple of spots in the Bible that allude to various classes of heavenly attendants (the "principalities" and "powers" are kinds of blessed angels). Paul was stating that, as great as heavenly angels may be, even they can't do us eternal harm.

Christ Above The Angels

BLESSED ANGELS ASSUMED A noteworthy job in Jewish old stories, which gave them a job in giving the Law to Moses. Numerous individuals including a portion of the Jews who progressed toward becoming Christians-may have been on the fringe of worshiping the holy angels.

The letter to the Hebrews clarifies that Christ is superior to the holy angels, for He is the unique, Only Begotten, Son of God, the one celestial Mediator among God and humankind. Jews underlines that the holy angels themselves worship Christ, thus should every single person (1:4-14).

Angels Unawares

"BE NOT CARELESS TO entertain strangers: for consequently some have engaged holy angels unprepared" (Heb. 13:2). The creator of Hebrews had as a top priority the story Abraham engaging three heavenly attendants who, we accumulate, looked like typical people (Gen. 18:1-5) and who ate human sustenance. This story raises the likelihood that anybody we engage may be a holy angel in disguise.

In Flaming Fire

JESUS' SECOND COMING IS uplifting news for the individuals who have faith in Him, terrible news for the individuals who dismiss Him. Paul discussed Jesus' coming back to earth "from paradise with His compelling heavenly angels, in blazing flame getting revenge on the individuals who don't know God, and on the individuals who don't comply with the good news of our Lord Jesus Christ.

These will be punishment with everlasting destruction" (II Thess. 1:7-9). "Everlasting" here proposes that individuals who trust that hellfire is just impermanent aren't right, similar to those the individuals who have faith in annihilationism.

The Four Living Creatures

REVELATION 4 PICTURES FOR us the position of royalty room of paradise, in which are four "living creatures," each with six wings and "brimming with eyes around and inside" (v. 8). One of the creatures resembled a lion, the second like a calf, the third like a man, the fourth like a eagle.

Day and night they recited, "Holy, holy, holy, Lord God Almighty, Who was and will be and is to come!" (v. 8). Were these heavenly angels? Clearly truly, however not the ordinary, human-showing up blessed angels. They were like the seraphim in Isaiah's vision (Isa. 6), who additionally went to upon God and sang, "Holy, holy, holy." Their creature like appearances likewise proposes Ezekiel's "living creatures" (Ezek. 1;10), which were also secured with eyes.

The Book From An Angel

REVELATION IS THE ONLY book of the Bible that really claims to have been the aftereffect of a visit from a holy angel: "The Revelation of Jesus Christ, which God offered Him to show His servants - things which should in the blink of an eye happen.

What's more, He sent and implied it by His blessed angel to His servant John" (1:1). It is suitable that Revelation specifies a heavenly angel in its first verse: the book contains in excess of seventy references to blessed angels, more than some other book of the Bible.

Chapter

FOUR

Questions And Answers Concerning Angels

1: Have Angels Watched Over People Very Long?

As far back as Adam's time, a holy messenger was sent to protect the tree of life, (Gen. 3:24). God has constantly utilized heavenly angels to do His work. He sends them forward as ministering spirits.

2. Are Angels Interested In Our Safety?

When judgment was going to fall on Sodom and Gomorrah, God sent two holy angels to caution Lot and his family (Gen. 19:1). They were first so concerned, they went to Abraham. They took Lot by the hand and pulled him out of the city.

3. Does The Appearance Of An Angel Prove That One Has Been Living More Holy Than Another?

We can't state that Lot was carrying on with a holy life. He was narrow minded and common. A holy angel appeared to Hagar to save her life after she had fought with her mistress (Gen. 21:17-19). The holy angel met Jacob at Bethel when he was fleeing from Esau. He had deceived his brother, yet the Lord was anxious to protect him.

The way that you protect your child does not always imply that your child has always been obedient.

4. Does An Angel Ever Commission One To Minister?

A blessed angel appeared to Moses in the wilderness and instructed him to lead God's children out of bondage (Exodus 3:2-12). A heavenly angel came to Gideon and instructed him to convey the children of God from the persecution of the Midianites (Judges 6:12-22).

5. Does An Angel Ever Provide Food For The Hungry?

Once Elijah had conveyed a revival to a whole country. He was tired after he had devastated 950 false prophets. He kept running from Jezebel, after he had been bolstered by the ravens; after he had lived three and one-half years without an apportion book. He ended up frail and set down to rest. A blessed angel met him under the juniper tree. Nourishment from paradise was given to Elijah. This prophet went forty days on the strength of this heavenly food (I Kings 19:5-7). This was not a fast. Elijah feasted forty days.

6. Do Angels Fight For God's People?

Once the general population of God were dwarfed by the Syrian armed force. Hezekiah fell on his knees and prayed. He spread an undermining letter out before the Lord. God saw that His people were offended by the adversary. He saw that they were in risk.

In reply to Hezekiah's supplication, He sent a blessed angel. The heavenly angel slew 185,000 fighters (soldiers) in a single night. The dread of God happened upon whatever is left of them and they fled for their lives (Isaiah 37). Should somebody undermine you, whatever you do is spread it out before the Lord. The Lord sees; the Lord knows and the Lord hears.

7. Do Angels Foretell The Future?

Gabriel appeared to Mary and revealed to her she would bring forth the Christ child (Luke 1:26-38). He revealed to Zacharias that he would be the father of John the Baptist. He disclosed to him the sort of preacher John would be (Luke 1:11-19).

8. Does An Angel Ever Bring Judgment?

A heavenly angel revealed to Zacharias he would be idiotic (dumb) in light of the fact that he didn't trust the message (Luke 1:20). A holy angel pulverized 185,000 warriors for King Hezekiah. A holy angel destroyed Herod since he didn't give God the glory. Herod was eaten with worms (Acts 12:23).

They may show up inside or outside the congregation (church). Hagar was in the wilderness. Moses was in the wilderness. Gideon was sifting grain behind a wine press. Elijah was behind a tree. Peter was in prison. Paul was amidst a tempest on the sea. Zacharias was in church (Luke 1:26-38).

9. Do Angels Help People Who Break The Law?

A law was passed denying Daniel to pray. He supplicated at any rate. He was thrown into a sanctum (den) of lions for overstepping the law. A heavenly angel went into the den of lions with him. A heavenly angel secured this offender (Numbers 23:23). It was illegal for Peter to preach in the city. He trusted it was smarter to obey God than man. He went to jail for overstepping the law. A holy angel came and conveyed him (Acts 5:19). This holy angel instructed him to return and again preach.

10: Will An Angel Appear To A Man Who Does Not Have The Holy Ghost?

Cornelius did not have the Holy Ghost. He didn't know anything about the Holy Ghost. However, a blessed angel appeared to him and he was told to send men to Joppa. He sent Peter who came and trained him in the way. Incredible revival followed (Acts 10).

11: Are Angels Interested In The Holy Ghost Baptism?

This blessed angel was especially concerned. He needed the Gentiles to receive the Holy Ghost (Acts 10:7-22). As per his word Peter came and preached. Before he had completed all who heard were sanctified through water in the Holy Ghost (Acts 10:44). Blessed angels want to investigate the way that man can preach the gospel with the Holy Ghost sent down from paradise (I Peter 1:12).

12: Do Angels Hold The Door To Prisons?

Blessed angels are imprison breakers. They can break into detainment facilities. They needn't bother with a key, as we probably am aware a key. They may break any jail that may hold you. They have the master key. The blessed angel drove Peter out. The entryways opened voluntarily (Acts 12:10). Hundreds of years before men had the key to a seeing-eye entryway, heavenly angels had that mystery.

13: Do Angels Deliver Only The Righteous?

They are not committed to convey the ungodly, but rather they can if they want to do as such. A blessed angel came to convey Paul and Silas. He sent a quake. Paul's bonds were loosed and Silas was set free. Everybody in the jail was set free (Acts 16:26). God is as yet sovereign. He does what He pleases. He sees fit His own.

14: Do Angels Bring The Answers To Our Prayers?

That is their business. At the point when Paul was out amidst the sea in the tempest, a blessed angel appeared to him and disclosed to him all that every one of the men that were with him would be saved (Acts 27:23). Hagar and Ishmael were praying when a heavenly angel presented to them the appropriate response (Gen. 21:17).

15: Can The Natural Man See An Angel?

The natural man can't receive the things of God (I Cor. 2:14). No man has seen God whenever. God is spirit (John 1:18; John 4:24). A holy angel is a spirit (Heb. 1:13,14). You can't see a spirit with your common eyes. At the point when a blessed angel shows up, one individual may see him and another may not see him. Elisha asked that the Lord would open his hireling's eyes that he could see the holy angels that were simply overhead (II Kings 6:17).

Joshua did not see that a heavenly angel was close by as he was in the fight. God helped him to see the holy angel (Joshua 5:13). A holy angel stood in the way to shield Balaam from setting off to the wrong place to preach. Balaam's donkey saw the holy angel. As the blessed angel remained there, Balaam did not see him for quite a while (Num. 22:31). A donkey can discern holy angels superior to some insubordinate ministers.

16: Are Angels Like Human Beings?

Angels don't have physical bodies, however they may seem to individuals, as though they had physical bodies. At some point they may show up in their great eminence (Acts 10:30). A holy angel appeared to Daniel like a beryl. His face showed up as lightning, his eyes were as lights of fire, his arms and feet resembled cleaned metal or polished brass. His voice resembled the voice of a multitude (Dan. 10:6).

17: Why Do Angels Sometimes Appear Without Their Heavenly Glory?

This is a result of a few reasons. Generally a dread happens upon the person when a holy angel shows up. Some of the time holy angels may go about as mystery criminologists. They might not have any desire to make themselves known to specific people. For example, an explorer may drop by and request help.

His auto might be separated, or he might be out of gas. He may need a place to rest. You could possibly engage him. You may welcome him to remain and not know he is a heavenly angel (Heb. 13:2).

At the judgment he can witness against you for breaking the charge, "Be not absent minded to engage strangers." You will be judged as indicated by the books by your works.

18: Are Angels Of A Very High Order?

Adam was made a little lower than the angels (Psalms 8:45). There are different orders of angels.

19: Which Of Them Are Described As Having Wings?

Seraphims appeared to Isaiah with wings. They were the holy angels of the Lord. Their fundamental obligation is to announce the blessedness of the Lord (Isaiah 6:1-8). The Cherubims showed up with wings. They guard the throne of royalty of God (Ezekiel 1:4-25; Ezeliel 10:1-22; Rev. 4:6-8).

20: Are There Male And Female Angels?

They are spoken of in the masculine gender. The Lord's angels do not marry or give in marriage. In that sense they are not of either sex (Matt. 22:30) They have a celestial body. It appears that fallen angels may not be without sex (Gen. 6:1).

21: Are Angels Mortal Or Do They Have A Celestial Body?

Angels possess a supernatural body, therefore angels can never die (Luke 20:36).

22: Are Angels Many In Number?

They are innumerable (Heb. 12:22). There are too many to count. there are millions upon million of angels (Rev. 5:11).

23: What Are Some Of The Duties Of The Angels?

The lives of Christians would be in steady threat or danger if it were not for blessed angels. Evil spirits are more terrible than a lion prepared to assault us anytime. Angels are watching over all Christians prepared to secure them consistently every day and every night.

God gives His heavenly angels charge over us to hold us up with their hands. They even ensure us against hitting our feet upon rocks as we walk (Psalms 91:11,12).

Chapter
FIVE

More Questions And Answers Concerning Angels

24: Do Angels Act Wisely?

They are entirely professional in their dealings. They never sit around idly or act absurdly. They convey their message and go on their way. They never receive worship (Rev. 22:8,9). They in every case direct worship to God.

25: Do Angels work, According To The Word of God?

An angel that demonstrations or talks in opposition to God's assertion, you can cast him out (Gal. 1:8,9). You can put a revile on him, for he isn't sent by the Lord. Indeed, even Jesus won the fight by saying, "It is written."

26: Are Angels Intelligent?

We currently know partially. When we get to paradise, we will know as we are known (I Cor. 13:12). We will be as the holy angels in paradise (Luke 20:36). We go from truth to truth on this planet, but holy angels appear to get a handle all in all reality at one time.

27: Do Angels Possess Omniscient?

There are a few things holy messengers don't have the foggiest idea. They don't have a clue about the hour of Jesus' coming (Mark 13:32). They don't about this Christian experience which we appreciate. They want to investigate it (I Peter 1:12).

28: Do Angels Have Will Power?

A heavenly angel has more self discipline than man. He never alters his opinion nor steps back. He doesn't pause. He realizes what he embarks to do and does not change. Holy angels has the data he needs before he starts the activity. His choices are sure. Ninety-eight percent of man's issues is in his hesitation (or indecision).

When man truly settles on a choice, most of his issues are complete. Holy angels have none of these hesitations and issues.

28: How Fast Do Angels Travel?

Angels can go from earth to heaven, or from one end of the earth to the other in a single instant. They can go as fast as man can think.

29: Are Angels All Powerful?

That relies on the power God gives them (Jude 8:9). One blessed angel appeared to require support when he was conveying the solution to Daniel's supplication (Daniel 10). It showed up the holy angel that acted the hero had more power.

30: Do Some angels Have More Power Than Others?

The Angel Michael could do what other heavenly angels couldn't do (Daniel 10). One heavenly angel has capacity to tie Satan without anyone else's input and placed him into the bottomless pit (Rev. 12:1,2).

31: Can We Have More Than One Angel To Help Fight Our Battles?

Jesus said that we could do the works that He did (John 12:14). He could have called down a large number of blessed angels to help Him at one time (Matt. 26:32).

32. Who Is Michael?

He is one of the princes that stands for Israel and with other blessed angels he will drive Satan and his bad angels out of paradise (Rev. 12). Michael needed to do with the resurrection of the dead (Daniel 12:1,2; Jude 2).

33: Who Is Gabriel?

Gabriel is the angel who had to do with God's work of redemption. Gabriel accompanied the understanding of Daniel's vision concerning the Gentile kingdom (Daniel 8:15-17). He is the holy angel who deciphered the future for Daniel (Daniel 9:20-27; Luke 11:11-20).

34: Does Gabriel Reveal The Future?

He informed Zacharias concerning the birth of John who was to be the precursor of the Savior (1:13). He remains within the sight of God (v. 19). He predicted the future when he revealed to Zacharias he would be moronic (dumb) nine months due to his disbelief (v. 20).

35: Does Each Child Have A Guardian Angel?

Jesus said there were blessed angels who dependably see the face of the Father which is in paradise (Matt. 18:10). A guardian heavenly angel is assigned out every child. Jesus said except if we end up converted and become as a little child, we will not see the kingdom of paradise (Matt. 18:3).

There is a genuine punishment assigned to any individual who hurts a little child. That is the thing that God considers children. You may state, "By what method would children be able to die?" God in His benevolence takes a few youngsters at an early age to shield them from experiencing childhood in sin and going to hell (I Kings 14).

36: How Long Will An Angel Watch Over A Child?

It will be there as long as the child makes it welcome. At the point when a child goes to the period of responsibility (age of accountability) and goes into transgression (sin), the holy angel isn't obligated to protect the child. A few young people debase themselves and go into spots where heavenly attendants would not follow them. They unreservedly turn themselves over to the fallen angel's of Satan.

37: If An Angel Watches Over A Child, Why Would You Pray For The Child?

There's a contrast between the children of godly guardians and the children of evil guardians. If there was no distinction, for what reason would a portion of the guardians bring the youngsters to Jesus and have Him to bless them? The spirit of the youngster will be saved, but wickedness can come upon them if the guardians don't pray (Ezek. 9:1-4).

A few youngsters are taken into irreverent houses where the devil's angels abide; where malady and passing rule. The child might be in danger. The Lord even may allow the child to go to paradise to get him out of wrongdoing (sin) and illness, and given him a chance to miss hell. The child is not responsible for this.

38: Are Angels Only With Children?

Everyone who fears the Lord has a heavenly angel that encampeth around him. That isn't all. The blessed angel is there to deliver him from the snare of the foe (Psalms 34:7).

39: Do Angels Protect Only People Who Live A Perfect Life?

The blessed angel won't abandon us when we make a mistake or yield to temptations in a moment of weakness. Hagar's conduct was not actually right. It appeared she had envy in her heart against her mistress, Sarah. However blessed angels acted to rescue her and her child when they were disregarded in the wild to starve. Maybe they appealed to God and He sent the heavenly angel to them. Maybe she did some repenting (Gen. 21:16-19).

Jacob did not in every case carry on with a decent life. He made the best choice in the wrong way. He knew the claim of birthright was his, yet he acquired it in an insidious technique. I guess he did some supplicating and repenting when his brother Esau was seeking his life.

One night he stated, "Without a doubt the Lord was in this place and I knew it not." He saw a ladder with the holy angels ascending and descending on it. This demonstrates God sends His blessed angels to ensure us when we are not aware of it (Heb. 13:2).

40: Is This The Only Time That Jacob Met An Angel?

It appears it was a typical thing for him to have blessed angels to encourage him. One night he wrestled throughout the night with a blessed angel. He did some confessing. He declined to give the holy angel a chance to hurl until the point when he got the appropriate response and acquired the blessing. Every one of the issues among him and his sibling were tackled (Gen. 32:28).

Jacob said the heavenly angel had redeemed his life (Gen. 48:16). He trusted the same heavenly angel would protect his descendants. He had the blessing of Abraham with him. We do as well (Gal. 4:13).

41: Will Angels Help In A Moment Of Weakness?

Elijah was strong. He delivered revival to a country. He brought down fire from paradise. He pulverized 950 false prophets. When he was exhausted and running for his life, running from that insidious woman Jezebel, he appealed to God; for the Lord to end his life. Exactly around then, a heavenly angel brought sustenance to strengthen him. God said we are men of like passion (I Kings 19:48). We may have the triumph one day and need strength the following day. A blessed angel is adjacent to supply the additional strength.

Chapter
SIX

Additional Questions And Answers Concerning Angels

42: Do Angels Do Our Fighting Without Our Knowing It, Sometimes?

Elisha knew there was a band of blessed angels over him, but the servant did not know it. He supplicated that the eyes of the servant would be open, that he could see those that were for them far outnumbered the ones against them (II Kings 6:17).

43: Do People Who Are Not Christians Sometimes See Angels?

King Nebuchadnezzar was known as an evil King. He saw somebody in the fiery furnace with the three Hebrew young men, as unto the Son of God (Daniel 3:25). At that point he proclaimed that God had sent a blessed angel and delivered the ones who confided in Him (Daniel 3:28). Holy angels can uncover themselves to sinners if they so desire.

44: Do Angels Go Into Dangerous Places?

Daniel was put into a risky, dangerous place. I would state it was a hazardous place to be tossed into a den of hungry lions. Lions have been known to defeat elephants and tigers. The lion is the king of the jungle. However a blessed angel was sent to close the lions' mouths that they would not hurt Daniel (Daniel 6:22).

In the event that you can close lions' mouths, you are strong. If the blessed angels can close the mouths of lions, they would then be able to be with me in some other sort of danger.

45: Do Angels Warn Us Of Things To Come?

Gabriel revealed to Joseph that Herod would attempt to murder the child Jesus. He advised Joseph to escape to Egypt. After Herod was dead, the heavenly angel revealed to Joseph it would be OK for him to come back to his country (Matt. 2:13-20).

46: Can A Person Be Guided By Angels?

Gabriel advised Joseph to accept Mary as his significant other, that the child was of the Holy Ghost. A holy angel appeared to Peter in jail. He guided him to tie on his shoes and he guided him out of the jail (Acts 12).

47: Can Angels Open Doors Without A Key?

We don't realize what sort of key, however it appears they have the way to each circumstance. As Peter strolled alongside the holy angel, the way to the jail simply opened. Whenever Peter and John were in prison, since they had preached in the city, a blessed angel let them out and instructed them to go preach again (Acts 5:20).

48: Can God Deliver The Answer To Our Prayers By An Angel?

Out on the sea amidst a tempest Paul and 276 men were about to be ship wrecked. A blessed angel remained by him and disclosed to him that he and every one of the men on board would be saved (Acts 27:21-25). A similar assurance can be sent to me by a holy angel.

49: Are Certain Angels Assigned To Certain Ones?

It appears that they are, as indicated by Acts 12:15. It appeared that the general population in the early church knew and anticipated that every individual would have a heavenly angel assigned to him. The general population appealed to God for Peter to be delivered from jail. When he went to the door and thumped they thought it was his blessed angel.

Assume a man intentionally goes into transgression (sin). At that point the guardian angel may withdraw. God can pull back His assurance or protection from a nation, a city or a person. After Israel purposely started to enjoy sin, the heavenly angel of the Lord would never again drive out the foe from before them. They went into bondage (Judges 2:1-3). The adversary moved toward becoming thistles or thorns in their sides.

50: Are We In The Presence Of Angels At All Times?

It appears to be sure that we are (Psalm 34:7). Solomon realized that heavenly angels were tuning in to words that we are stating consistently (Eccles. 5:6). The heavenly angels can record what we say. Our words can demolish us. In the event that we can repent of the transgressions (sins) which the heavenly angels record on the books, at that point indeed, they will be blotted out (Acts 3:19).

51: What Kind Of Good Deeds Can Be Recorded?

Any good deed might be recorded. For instance, whenever you are devoted in supplication, it very well may be recorded. You can remain in the gap and make up the support and hold back the judgments. A blessed angel observes this (Ezek. 2:1-9).

52: Who Has Sure Protection By An Angel?

All that fear the Lord are assured of protection. All that stay in the mystery place of the Most High are given this assurance. They will withstand under the shadow of the Almighty (Pslam 91:10-13). The Lord will give His blessed angels charge over us.

53: Are We Sometimes Stopped By An Angel?

A Certain sister of my former church, started to reach above her head to get some eggs out the hen's nest. A divine person stopped and caught her hand. Then she observed a snake was coiled up int the next above. This divine person had been watching over her and protected her.

54: Do Angels Associate Closely With Us?

It appears that they trust us excessively. The mystery of the Lord is with them that fear Him, however there are sure mysteries that are not given to specific individuals. At the point when Jacob approached the blessed angel for his name, the heavenly angel declined to impart that mystery to Jacob (Gen. 32:29). They more often than not do what they are sent to do and after that rapidly withdraw, at any rate from our sight.

55: Are Angels Diety?

Holy angels nearly take after God, since they convey the glory of God with them. Some that have seen heavenly angels, have thought they have seen God (Judges 6:22,23). Their words are viewed as the expressions of God. They do not talk vain words. They talk as the oracles of God.

We are told to speak as God's oracles as opposed to clowning and quipping constantly and telling things that are not true (I Peter 4:11).

56: Are Angels To Be Worshiped?

A genuine heavenly angel will reject worship. He will direct the worship to God. There were individuals in the New Testament that worshiped holy angels. Paul condemned this practice (Col. 2:18). After John had been educated within the sight of God for quite a long time, despite everything he didn't fight the temptation to tumble down and worship a holy angel, the nearness of the heavenly angel was so great. The heavenly angel declined to be worshiped (Rev. 22:8,9). In Judges 13:16 Samson's mother attempted to sacrifice to a blessed angel and this sacrifice was refused.

57: Will Prayers Dispatch An Angel?

Heavenly angels revealed to Lot that they couldn't do anything until the Lot was out of the city. It was not a direct result of Lot or his family's good life or supplications, it was a direct result of the intervention of loyal Abraham (Gen. 18:23-28). Lot waited. He kept down. The daughters demonstrated they were not very righteous. Lot's better half (wife) looked back to her belongings and turned to a pillar of salt. A blessed angel took Lot by the hand and hauled him out of the city.

58: How Can We Keep The Angels With Us?

We should pursue intently as did Peter when he left jail. We should wrestle in prayer as did Jacob. We should heed the warnings as lot did. We should not go places a blessed angel would not dare tread.

59: Do Angels Come After Departing Saints?

There are numerous such testimonies from Christians who go from this life. A few people pass that off as dreams or hallucinations. Jesus recounted a specific beggar. He didn't pass it off as an illustration. He said there was a sure rich man and a beggar. The rich man kicked the died and went to damnation (hell).

Most likely the rich man was conveyed there by the devil's angels. At the point when the poor man kicked the bucket (died), the holy angels of God came to him and carried him to heaven, which was called Abraham's bosom (Luke 16:22).

60: Will Angels Carry You Away?

Indeed, there are one of two arrangements of heavenly attendants which will do as such. It will probably be the heavenly angel that strolls with you in this life. It appears to be sure that God's holy angel will divert you to paradise and that the fallen angel (Satan attendants) will divert some to a position of everlasting disdain (hellfire), where there will be no more revival, water or little children. Be sure to stay away from places where the devil's angels are, and where God's angels dare not walk.

61: Do Angels Destroy The enemy?

One angel slew 185,000 one night. The nation of Assyria came against the nation of Juda. Hezekiah prayed. An angel fought and won the battle for him (Isaiah 37:26-38).

62: What Else Do Angels Do After One Dies?

The Archangel Michael, is by all accounts associated with the resurrection of the righteous dead. He was there to guarantee the collection of Moses body (Jude 9). Michael is associated with the general resurrection (Daniel 12:1,2). About the season of the resurrection there will be a war in the elements between the Lord's heavenly angels and the devil's unholy angels.

Michael will lead the battle (Rev. 12:7). At the point when Jesus accompanies his heavenly angels, the righteous will ascend to meet Him. He will send the blessed angels with a shout, the great shout of the trumpet. They will gather His elect from the four winds of the earth (Matt. 25:29-31). Michael will most likely be the leader of the band of holy angels.

63: How Will Angels Do Such A Tremendous Task As This?

Maybe the blessed angel will raise the one from the dead that he has secured amid his lifetime (Jude 9). The devil's angel's may even attempt to stop the resurrection of the righteous dead, however the holy angels of the Lord will win the battle. The righteous dead will take on a body like unto Jesus' glorified body and they will ascend to meet Jesus in the air (Phil. 3:21).

64: What Will Then My Angel Do?

Maybe he will make gravity lose its hold. At that point, I will rise to meet my Lord in the air. So will we ever be with the Lord (I Thess. 5:17). I will meet the Christians from everywhere in the air. They will originate from China, Russia, Africa, England and all aspects of the world. Not in any case the heavenly angels know the hour of Jesus Coming (Matt. 24:36).

65: Will Old Testament Saints Be Brought In?

It is apparent that the blessed angels of God battle the angels of Satan. There is an incredible profound clash between these angels (Daniel 10:12,13). We are allowed to see into the inconspicuous world in this part. A high positioning angel from Satan opposed a angel from God for three weeks. Michael, the lead celestial host (the archangel), came to aid the battle and won the fight. He acted the hero. God loves me as much as He did Daniel.

66: Do Some Angels Have More Power Than Others?

A few holy angels have higher position and more power than other heavenly angels. One heavenly angel has power to put one foot upon the land and the other upon the ocean, lift his hand and swear unto Him that liveth for all eternity that time will be never again (Rev. 10:3). Another heavenly angel has power to close the mouths of lions (Daniel 6:22).

Another holy angel has power to open the entryway for a few ministers praying (Acts 5:19,20). Another heavenly angel has power to tie Satan and placed him into the bottomless pit (Rev. 20:1-5).

67: Will We Be As Angels In Heaven?

We will have a body like unto Jesus' celebrated body (Phil. 3:21). We will resemble Him for we will see Him to be as He is

(I John 3:2). Here and there we will be as blessed angels (luke 20:36). We won't wed nor give in marriage. We will serve Jesus and love Him. Most likely we will accomplish something other than sitting on the waterway banks or playing a harp.

That sounds like a languid man's paradise. I would not think about sitting on the bank of the stream. I need to be dynamic. We will serve (Heb. 1:14; Luke 20:36). There might be different universes. Perhaps I will be sent to deliver somebody from the lion's den, from a prison or from a red hot furnace. That would be paradise for me, just to be helpful.

68: Do Angels Ever Die?

In the resurrected life, we are equal to the angels. We will be children of the resurrection. We will be in the family of God. We cannot die. Angels do not die (Luke 20:36).

69: What Does God Have Against The Fallen Angels?

God made arrangement ahead of time for man's redemption. He previously had an arrangement of redemption for man. In this arrangement He gives us power over all the power of the fallen angel. This is through the atonement. I have power over all the power of the fallen angel through Jesus. Through Jesus no power in the earth, under the earth or in paradise can vanquish us (Romans 8:37-39). Jesus was the Lamb slain from the foundation of the world (Rev. 13:8).

70: How Can We Know The Bad Angels?

Through the endowment of the discerning of spirits we can know the contrast between great holy angels and terrible evil angels (I Cor. 12:10). Terrible angels can come to us as a angel of light (II Cor. 11:14).

Heavenly angels are spirits (Heb. 1:14). We require discerning of spirits to recognize them. Paul said for us not to trust spirits that come to present to us a message (II Thess. 2:2).

71: What Must We Do When An Angel Comes To Us With A Message?

We should do a same thing that Jesus did. We should state, "It is written," (Matt. 4:4). If a holy angel is from paradise discloses to you something, that it doesn't make the grade regarding the sacred writing, put a revile on the heavenly angel and cast him out (Gal. 1:8,9).

72: Will The Struggle Between God's Angels And The Devil's Angels Last Long?

If you fear the Lord, you have the holy angel of the Lord with you (Psalm 34:7). The battle won't keep going long. The God of Peace will wound Satan in the blink of an eye under your feet (Romans 16:20). You have power over all the power of the devil. Nothing shall by any means harm you (Luke 10:19). We are more than champions. When principalities or angels attempt to isolate us from the love of God, in Christ Jesus our Lord we have the triumph (Romans 8:38,39).

We will tread on snakes. We have power over all the power of Satan (Luke 9:1). All fallen angels implies huge villains, little demons, poor fiends, rich villains - all demons of each kind.

73: Why Must We Fight A Continual Fight Against Satan And His Angels?

We should battle so the gospel will have free course. What number of houses of worship are bound tight, adversary spirits have ceased the stream of God's spirit until the point that the general population don't supplicate. The evangelist has his situation is practically hopeless. The gospel does not have free course in these churches.

74: How Must We Fight?

Daniel gave us a model. He asked that intercessory petition would open ways to the gospel, and would convey saintly powers from paradise to war against Satan's powers. Satan remains before the blessed angel of the Lord to oppose him. As somebody implores, he can state, "The Lord rebukes thee" (Zech. 3:1-3).

75: Where Do We Get Our Power Against Satan's Angels?

When Jesus came to confront the cross, He recognized what it was. He stated, "Now is the judgment of this world: Now will the prince of the world be thrown out; Now is the prince of this world judged" (John 12:31; John 16:11). Lawful authority was stripped from Satan at Calvary. Jesus stated, "I observed Satan as lightning, tumble from paradise" (Luke 10:18). The genuine heavenly angels of God remain to help us and to tell us our rights in Jesus' name. Jesus drove the devil's unholy angels hostage and offered power to bind them (Ephesians 4:8; Matt. 18:19; Luke 10:19).

76: Do Angels Need Our Cooperation?

Holy angels must have our collaboration if they battle for us. Daniel intervened in petition as the blessed angels battled for him as he stayed the course of faith (Daniel 10:11,12). The fighting of the Christian has a vital impact in the fight to oust the power of Satan (Ephesians 6:12).

We and God's blessed angels are partners in the contention against Satan (Eph. 6:12). We should arm ourselves with the whole protective armor of God. Jesus could have called twelve armies of sacred holy angels to have helped Him (Matt. 26:53). He said we can do the same thing (John 14:12).

77: If We Have These Weapons, Why Then Do We Need Angels?

Holy angels of God battle against Satan's unholy angels. There is an spiritual warfare going in the components above. Satan's angels will endeavor to shield our supplications from going through. Satan will attempt to assault us in any capacity he can. While Jesus was praying in the Garden of Gethsemane, a heavenly angel showed up and fortified Him (Luke 42:23). As He seems to be, so are we in this world (I John 4:17).

78: When Will The Battle Above Us Be Ended?

Michael and the blessed angels will come and battle against the devil and his unholy angels. They will pursue the devil and his angels out of the elements above us, where they presently have their central station (Rev. 12:8-12). That is in the precise not so distant future. Satan knows his time is short. That is the reason he has incredible rage. That is the reason he is setting up such a battle. That is the reason we require the assistance from God's heavenly angels that encamp around about us.

79: How Will Satan And His Angels Be Overcome?

The holy people of God will contribute to this. We should coordinate with the blessed angels. We will conquer the fallen angel by the blood of the Lamb and the Words of our testimony (Rev. 12:11).

80: Is It A Fact That We Play A Part Against Satan's Angels?

Angels of Satan realize that they are a vanquished enemy. They know they can't defeat us if we come against them in the Name of Jesus in faith. The Word of God evidently expresses that we shall judge angels (I Cor. 6:11). Almost certainly we will have a part in throwing Satan and his unholy angels into the bottomless pit.

81: How Can We Perform Such A Task As This?

That is the place the blessed messenger of God comes in. Every one of us have a guardian heavenly angel. Our holy angel is prepared and willing, holding up to shield us from Satan's angels. He will step forward and bind the detestable angel that assaults us. Presumably our blessed angel will take the unholy angels that battle against us. He will be thrown into the bottomless pit with the malevolent chief angel (Satan). Hence we will win our last triumph, the triumph of all things considered. We will win the victory!

82: Does The Pastor Of Each Church Have An Angel With Him?

Indeed, in the event that it is God's congregation and God has put the individuals in it (I Cor. 12:28). If God has put the pastor over the congregation, He has given him a heavenly angel to battle his fights. John made this plain when he revealed to us that every one of the seven houses of worship of Asia had a blessed angel with them (Rev. 1,2,3). A blessed angel is a spirit (Heb. 1:14). Every pastor must have this ministering spirit with him, if he is to do what God has offered him to do.

A pioneer of one of the false churches would without a doubt have one of the fallen angel's holy messengers with him. We should petition God for the pastors as Satan sends his unholy angels along to attempt to get every pastor to bargain and let down the standard of holiness and righteousness.

83: Is An Angel A Person?

Truly, a blessed angel is a person.. A person who does not must have a body with tissue, blood and bones. A spirit does not have substance, blood or bones. A blessed angel is a spirit. A spirit is a person as per the dictionary. God is a spirit (John 4:24). However, God is a person (Heb. 1:3), No man has seen God at any time (I John 4:12). However, we may see him with our spiritual eyes (John 14:9).

84: Can We Not Just Depend Upon The Gifts Of The Spirit?

It appears that heavenly angels have something to do with the manifestation of the gifts. They are working through the same spirit. At the point when Paul was in a tempest confronting wreck, all expectation was taken away. It appeared to be sure 276 men would go down to their death. Simply then Paul got the affirmation from God that every one of them would be saved.

Not one of them would be lost (Acts 27:24). This assurance from God is the endowment of faith in task. Paul got the assurance while he was praying. The appropriate response was "God has given all of you them that sail with thee." This was past tense. For this situation, a blessed angel brought this assurance.

85: Do Angels Really Answer Our Prayers?

For the situation specified over this was valid. God sends His heavenly angels on such errands. They deliver the affirmation to our supplications. Here and there we are gone when the holy angel arrives. A man imagined that he saw a few packages in paradise. When he asked what they were, the Lord disclosed to him that they were undelivered answers to prayers.

The ones praying were gone when the blessed angels touched base with the appropriate response. The blessed angels came back with the undelivered gifts. The packages in the dream are images of unanswered prayers.

86: Does God Have Many Angels?

At the point when John investigated paradise he saw ten thousand times ten thousand, a huge number of blessed angels (Rev. 11:5). He tallied to one hundred million. He quit counting about, investigated space and saw thousands. They are an incalculable number (Heb. 12:22; Rev. 5:11).

87: Does An Angel Want You To Be Cheerful?

If you are constantly disheartened or discouraged, you have the devil's angel's with you. For a heavenly angel of God to encourage you, he necessitates that you be cheerful (Acts 27:22). It requires faith. In the event that you have faith, you are not dismal or debilitated. Your acclaim, your praise is the incense that ought to climb up to the position of authority of God throughout the day, consistently (Heb. 13:15; Eph. 5:2).

If you offer incense with your supplications, you will get results. A holy angel stands adjacent to the sacrificial table (altar) trusting that praise will climb up with your prayers (Rev. 8:3). He takes some fire from the holy place and blends it with the praise. He throws it to earth. There are voices, there is a shaking, there is a revival (Rev. 8:3,4).

Upon the day of Pentecost praise went up to God. Fire was blended with it. As it was thrown down to earth there were voices and there was an extraordinary revival (Acts 2:1-4). Whenever Paul and Silas were in prison they blended praises with their supplications. There was all of a sudden an incredible seismic tremor (earthquake) (Acts 16:26). Obviously the holy angel shook the entryways of that jail. There was an extraordinary revival that occurred. Individuals were saved, healed and baptize that night.

No wonder that God says for us to make our requests known with thanksgiving (Phil. 4:6). Let all things be managed without mumbling and whining (Phil. 2:14). Of all things don't mumble and gripe to God and call that supplicating. The devil's angels want you to do that.

88: Do Angels Believe In A Holy Life?

They have faith in and practice a holy life. They are blessed holy angels (Rev. 14:10). Holy angels don't sin. They come to reward judgment upon the general population that don't obey with the good news of the Lord Jesus Christ (II Thess. 1:7-9). The heavenly angels reported that Jesus would save individuals from their sins and not in their sins (Matt. 1:21).

89: Does It Take Discerning Of Spirits To See Angels?

God divides the gifts as He will (I Cor.12:11). Now and again God gives us a chance to see the inconspicuous hosts that are battling for us. They are there whether we see them or not. Elisha saw them, yet his servant did not. God opened the servant's spiritual eyes and he saw them; that there were more that were for them than that were against them (II Kings 6:17).

In the event that we have the discerning of spirits we will realize that there is a fight between two inconspicuous powers. We will likewise realize that they that be for us be more than those against us.

90: Do Angels Sleep?

A Spiritual being does not require sleep. The common, natural body needs sleep. While Jacob was sleeping, a band of blessed angels was ascending and descending on a ladder from earth to paradise. He said God was in that place and he knew it not (Gen. 28:12). Jacob was in a daze. His brother was seeking his life.

In the event that you are in a bad position, why stress? On the off chance that the blessed angels will remain conscious why not simply go ahead and sleep and rest? Nathanael saw the blessed angels ascending and descending on Jesus (John 1:51). As the Father sent Jesus, even so sends He us (John 20:21). Perhaps every one of the blessed angels needed the respect of being Jesus' body protect (body guard). They maybe needed to change moves and work certain hours.

91: Are We In The Presence Of Angels Now?

They are whether we want them or not. God did not say they encamps around about them that feel well, but around all that fear God (Psalm 37:4). When we take a marriage pledge, we take it within the sight of God and the blessed angels. Holy angels witness it and record it. When we are ordained to preach it happens within the sight of good heavenly angels or awful unholy angels persistently. Try not to do anything that will make blessed heavenly angels flee from you. It is important to be blessed in the event that you need to keep company with sacred holy angels. Live holy, walk holy, and dress holy.

92: How Do Angels Look?

They don't generally show up in the totality of their glory. Now and then they show up as men. Some may confuse them with men (Heb. 13:2). At different occasions their face resembles lightning. Their face is relatively similar to the face of God (Judges 13:22). Their pieces of clothing are white like snow (Matt. 2:3).

Men fall like dead men before them. Men shake since fear falls upon them. The men looked on Stephen as he was stoned to death. His face looked the essence of a holy angel (Acts 6:15). Heavenly angels don't shear their hair (I Cor. 7:10).

93: Do Angels Believe In The Holy Ghost Baptism?

They want to investigate reality that men preach the good news of the Holy Ghost sent down from paradise (I Peter

1:12). A blessed angel appeared to Cornelius and instructed him to send men to Joppa. He needed Peter to come disclose to them what they should do to get the Holy Ghost (Holy Spirit) (Acts 10:7-22). At the point when Peter came and instructed them, they were all so devoted they received the Holy Ghost. A blessed angel might be sent to you or he may educate an evangelist to come to you to train you how to get the Holy Ghost (Acts 3:14). The blessed angel did not go to the overseers. He went straightforwardly to Cornelius. (When you give your life to Jesus Christ, He provides you the Holy Spirit).

94: Does An Angel Ever Compliment Us?

Once a blessed angel came and sat down under an oak tree. He conversed with a child who was behind a wine press, sifting wheat. Gideon was there in light of the fact that the Midianites were removing God's childrens' belongings and nourishment (food) from them. The blessed angel revealed to Gideon that the Lord was with him. He was a powerful man of valor. It is honored inclination when a blessed angel compliments us.

95: Do Angels Work Miracles?

A holy angel directed Gideon to offer a sacrifice to the Lord. He instructed him to lay flesh and cakes on the stones. The holy angel advanced his staff and touched the sacrifice. There emerged fire out of the stones and expended the flesh and cakes (Judges 6:21). There is no miracle a heavenly angel can't do in the event that we are stuck in an unfortunate situation and shout out to God in faith.

96: Will An Angel Tell You Where To Go To Win A Soul?

After Philip had numerous incredible revivals in Samaria and had preached a large number of the Samaritans, a holy angel advised Philip to go down toward the South, in the desert of Gaza. He met the Eunoch from Ethopia who was looking for after truth. Philip went up to him as he was reading in the chariot, and he preached to him and he had accepted with everything that is in him (Acts 8:26).

A blessed angel holds up today to guide you to some lost soul that is eager for God. You should will go out into the desert to that one hungry man. The blessed angel will come to protect you.

97: Will God Use The Angels In The Last Day Revival?

Clearly heavenly angels will work in collaboration with man as on account of Philip winning the Eunoch (Acts 8:36). The harvest is the apocalypse. The collectors are the holy angels (Matt. 13:39-41). Jesus will send his blessed angels. They will assemble out everything that annoy or offend. They will expel the tares from the wheat.

The tares will be bound up and consumed. Jesus will accompany His heavenly holy angels with a fire of flame and get revenge upon them that know not God and that obey not the good news of the Lord Jesus Christ (II Thess. 1:7-9). You should repent and comply with the gospel in the event that you need the heavenly angels to be for you rather than against you.

The heavenly angel will be with Jesus when He partitions the sheep from the goats (Matt. 25:31,32). You won't need Him to be embarrassed (ashamed) about you before the heavenly blessed angels (Mark 8:38). At that point you admit Him here and live holy and righteous. He will gather we all for the rapture (Matt. 24:31).

98: Do Angels Depend Upon Us?

Heavenly angels work for the most part through us. They help us. They rely on us to participate with them. They see conditions through us as we obey God in mediation. We are scenes (spectacles) to holy angels (I Cor. 4:9).

99: What Status Do Angels Hold?

Adam was made a little lower than the heavenly angels (Heb. 2:7). The blessed angels are lower than Jesus, the holy angels worship Jesus (Heb. 1:5-7). Holy angels all bow to Jesus (I Peter 3:22). They serve and obey Him (Heb. 2:5). Jesus took on the form of man for a period, it was just for our redemption.

100: Will An Angel Protect Us When We Are Being Cheated?

An Angel will do our battling for us and pursue our adversaries (Psalm 35:5). When Jacob withstood his father-in-law, since his father-in-law abused him, changed his wages, a heavenly angel ensured him. Laban conned him and changed his wages multiple times. He attempted to end his life.

He gave him the wrong wife after he had labored for a long time. A blessed angel remained by Jacob and redeemed him from fiendishness, evil (Gen. 48:16). Vengeance belongs to the Lord and he will repay.

101: How Did The Israelites Destroy All The Nations Around Them?

A heavenly angel did their battling for them and led them to the promised land (Exodus 23:20). They were directed to be careful with the blessed angel and not provoke him (23:21). God's name was in the holy angel. The holy angel went before Moses and instructed him (Exodus 32:34). Holy angels helped them to take hold of the promise, we also have blessed angels to encourage us.

102: Can An Angel Foretell The Future?

An Angel came to Manoah. He told this woman that she was infertile, yet would bare a child. He disclosed to her what to sustain the child. Her child, Samson, was a Nazarite. The blessed angel advised her not to give a razor a chance to fall upon his head. The heavenly angels are keen on us living holy lives.

103: Does An angel Have Power Over Fire?

Fire can't consume a heavenly angel. A heavenly angel went into the fire with the Hebrew young men. A blessed angel climbed back to paradise in a fire of flame (Judges 13:20). One blessed angel has control over flame (Rev. 12:18). He will cast the fire into the winepress of the fury of God. Blood will keep running up to the horses' harnesses. A heavenly angel appeared to Moses in a fire of flame in the consuming bush (Exodus 3:2).

104: Will An Angel Help Select A Wife?

I trust a holy angel will go before you and help you select the correct man or woman. A holy angel or the presence of

God came to me and demonstrated to me the woman I was to take as my better half. In the Bible, Isaac did not know his significant other's name before he hitched her even that long. A heavenly angel ran with Abraham's servant and helped him select a wife for Issac (Gen. 24:7). This is the reason the servant did not experience considerable difficulties picking a young lady to be Isaac's significant other.

105: Will Angels Go With Us Through Trials?

They went with Jesus and tended to Him on the Mount of Temptation (Matt.4:11). God knows how to convey the godly out of temptation (II Peter 2:9). He conveyed Lot by heavenly angels (Gen. 19:11). The heavenly angel destroyed the men with visual deficiency (blindness) who attempted to attack him. At the point when Abraham was enticed and tried even taking his own child's life, a heavenly angel called to him and let him know not to making it impossible to make the last, lethal stroke (Gen. 22:11).

106: Do Angels Rejoice When A Sinner Is Saved?

There is joy within the sight of holy angels when a sinner returns home (Luke 15:10). Your mom who has proceeded to be with the Lord is within the sight of heavenly angels, in the extraordinary billow of observers, and she may cheer when her very own child comes back to his mother's God. The petitions were addressed that she asked while she was on earth.

I trust holy angels additionally cheer. They sang and cheered when Jesus was conceived. They said he came to save his people from their sins (Matt. 1:21).

Chapter
SEVEN

Still Further, More Questions And Answers

107: Do Angels Weep?

Some think they are tragic and even sob for sinners that are lost. I would preferably trust holy angels are brimming with bliss. When you are brimming with happiness, and joy there is no space for pity in you. I perused how they are praising God ceaselessly in paradise (Rev. 7:11). They even fall on their faces praising God. We will be as holy angels in paradise (Luke 20:36). There will be fulness of joy in His presence (II Tim. 1:4). Misery and distress will then be finished.

108: What Do Angels Have To Do About Visions?

The holy angels deciphered the vision that Zacharias had seen (Luke 1). When we see dreams, we can rely on our heavenly angel giving us the elucidation. Commonly in the previous years God has given me visions. Now and then I would know the vision was from the Lord, however would not know the understanding. It was comprehended in Bible occasions that heavenly angels normally show up in visions (Luke 24:23).

The writer had numerous such encounters. Peter saw a heavenly angel. The blessed angel loosed him from jail, Peter still thought he had seen a vision (Acts 12:9).

109: Do Angels Send Us To Carry The Message?

The angel moved the obstacle from some women. He rolled back the stone and sat upon it. He knew whom Mary was seeking. He knew Jesus had risen. He sent Mary with the message of the resurrection. An angel may send you with the message. You may receive your call to preach by the visitation of an angel.

110: Are Angels Interested In Your Healing?

Blessed angels aid any way they can in helping individuals. They are utilized in conveying answers to our prayers. A holy angel descended every year and troubled the waters. The first individual that ventured into the water was healed (John 5:1-6).

111: Do Angels Only Record Bad Deeds?

They record all our good deeds. The Lord harkens and hears as we meet and talk regularly to each other. A book of rememberance is made notwithstanding when our thoughts are on the Lord (Mal. 3:16). We will be rewarded by our works (II Cor. 5:10).

112: Did Men Believe More In Angels In Bible Times Than They Do Today?

Men are pretty much indistinguishable in all ages. The Sadducees were a group that did not have belief in holy angels or supernatural occurrences. In this manner, they were tragic (sad), you see (Acts 23:8). The Pharisees trusted in blessed angels. At the point when God spoke from the components a portion of the general population rushed to trust a blessed angel spoke (John 12:29). When Peter was delivered from jail, the general population thought it was his heavenly angel (Acts 12:15).

113: Can We Expect An Angel To Destroy Our Enemy?

We can in the event that we pray. Once Hezekiah got a letter from an evil king. He spread the letter out before the Lord. The Lord can read, you know. The Lord assured King Hezekiah that through the endowment of faith he would be shielded. That night a blessed angel slew 185,000 troopers, basically the leaders (II Chron. 32:21; II Kings 19:35). This instructs us to take every one of our inconveniences, threats and dangers to God.

God sees and hears; He wants to think about it and He gets it. We learn here that God's blessed angels don't wish to annihilate any a larger number of men than would normally be appropriate.

114: Do Angels Also Bring Judgment?

Holy angels showed up in human form to advise Lot of the coming devastation to their city. When the men of the city came and attempted to molest them, the holy angels destroyed them with visual impairment (blindness). The holy angels have something that is more prominent than any nerve gas firearm. The heavenly angels can destroy your adversary with visual deficiency so they can't see to assault you. No weapon that is formed against thee will prosper (Gen. 19:16,17).

115: Should We Ignore A Warning From An Angel?

Lot's significant other is a case of one who does not regard or heed the warning. He advised her to escape from the city and not look back. When she did, she turned to a pillar of salt. Jesus, in talking about the coming judgment on this planet said for us to remember Lot's wife (Luke 17:31).

116: Does There Come A Time When The Angel Departs?

The heavenly angel needed to leave Lot's wife since she continued in insubordination (disobedience). They are tolerant and quiet, however in the event that we oppose and revolt or rebel there comes a period that they will pull back themselves. They will take their protection from around you. Then they are turned against you.

117: Do Angels Help Us At Times We Do Not See Them?

While Balaam was out of the will of God and going to revile God's people, a blessed angel showed up in the way to stop him. So merciful is God that when an evangelist fails God and starts to put a revile on God's people, or to skin the sheep, here and sometimes a blessed angel will show up in his way to square him from further destruction (Numbers 22:12).

Balaam did not understand it, but rather the blessed angel was keeping him from going further into obliteration. The creature (jackass) saw the heavenly angel, however Balaam did not. At last, God opened Balaam's eyes so he saw the heavenly angel. This saved Balaam's life.

Blessed angels are spirits. The minister was so licentious and cool that he couldn't discern spirits. He didn't have as much acumen of spirits as did the moronic creature on which he was riding. We have such lewd evangelists today, they can't discern spirits. He that is in the flesh can't please God (I Cor. 2:14). They that love God must love Him in the spirit (John 4:23).

118: Can Angels Turn Against Us?

It appears Balaam had continued in going on, in any case. He would have been slaughtered on the spot. The blessed angel was in his way with his sword drawn. possibly his very own guardian holy angel had betrayed him. He would have battled against him rather than for him. At a later time Balaam was murdered for forming up against God's people (Joshua 13:22).

119: Would The Angel Ever Fight Against Us?

After Saul defied the Lord and wound up rebellious, insubordinate, God rejected him (I Sam. 15:23). God turned into his foe (I Sam. 28:16). Rather than the heavenly angel of the Lord ensuring a man, he may really pursue him (Psalm 35:4-6). The heavenly angel takes God's part. He battles on God's side.

At the point when Saul ventured on the devil's side, he was God's adversary. When we are on the fallen angel's side, we at that point in battle against the holy angel of the Lord. If we are not for the Lord we are against him (Matt. 15:30).

120: Which Angels Sinned?

Lucifer, the archangel, sinned and was cast out of heaven, according to most Christian people's belief (Isaiah 14:12-20).

121: How Did Lucifer Sin?

Lucifer was lifted up by pride. He needed to lift up his position of authority over the stars of God. He needed to resemble the most high (Isa. 14:13,14). No one but Christ can be equivalent to God. Christ will sit on his father's throne (Rev. 3:21).

122: Was Lucifer Perfect?

t appears at one time he was sinless and impeccable (Ezek. 28:15). At that point God discovered evildoing in him. He was lifted up proudly. He had beauty, appeal and reverence of paradise. He was lifted up in light of beauty (Ezek. 28:17).

123: What Happened After He Fell?

He became the prince of darkness; he became the god of this world. He can transform himself into an angel of light. He is the prince and the power of the air. He is the accuser of the brethren. He accuses them before God day and night.

124: Does An Angel Stand Against The Enemy?

As the children of Israel walked over the Red Sea, the adversary was behind them relatively getting them. Around three million individuals were walking by foot. What impeded Pharoah's armed force from getting them? They were in chariots. The heavenly angel of God that went before God's people, expelled and went behind them (Gen. 14:19). The holy angel shone a light for God's people. He made it dark for the Egyptians. The wheels fell off the chariots. They were ousted into the sea.

125: Would An Angel Want You To Go To A Fortune Teller?

He won't go with you. You are not ensured that you do these things and are going on the fallen angel's region. King Ahaziah sent messages to Beelzebub to ask that he would recoup from his disease (II Kings 1:2). A blessed angel informed

Elijah regarding it. He advised Elijah to meet the dispatchers and send them back with a message from God. The heavenly angel sent word that the king would die.

Envoys small sent to pulverize Elijah, yet Elijah called fire down from paradise and demolished them. A holy angel probably been doing this for Elijah, in light of the fact that the heavenly angel all of a sudden advised Elijah to go with the messengers for a meeting with the king (II Kings 1:15).

126: Can An Angel Rebuke?

A blessed angel came and advised the general population they were not to make a union with the occupants of the land, but should toss down their sacrificial stones (altars). He said they had done every one of these things that he let them know not to do. He said he had brought them out of Egypt, however would not drive out the adversary any longer since they had been defiant (rebellious, disobedient) (Judges 2:13).

Every one of the general population lifted up their voices and sobbed. It's anything but a lovely inclination when the heavenly angel that has been battling for you turns against you, rebukes you and start battling against you. The heavenly angel ordered a curse on Meraz in light of the fact that the general population did not come to help fight the Lord's battle (Judges 5:23). He can rebuke us for our sin of disregard, or neglect (Heb. 2:1-4).

127: Does An Angel Carry A Sword?

A few places in the Bible we find that blessed angels carried swords. One time we discover a holy angel stood prepared to demolish individuals all over the bank of Israel. After David repented, the Lord told the holy angel to secure (put away) the sword (I Chron. 21:12-30). If you repent the heavenly angel of the Lord will put away the sword. He will battle for you instead of against you.

128: What Will Happen To Fallen Angels?

They will be thrown into hell fire with Satan (Matt. 25:4). Hell fire is set up for Satan (Head Evil Angel, Lucifer). It was not set up for you, but rather on the off chance that you follow him (Satan) you will follow him to hell, for that is the place he is going (Rev. 20:1,2). 68

129: Did Lucifer Pull Down Angels With Him?

Indeed they followed Lucifer (He wound up known as "Satan"). We don't know what number of angels he pulled down, however we know God still has an extraordinary number of heavenly angels (Rev. 5:11). We are told there are a few angels that did not keep their first estate (Jude 6).

It appears Lucifer (Satan) was not fulfilled to fall himself, but rather he won the support of other angels and had them to rebel against God. Maybe he made them a few promises as he did to Eve. Every one of us have power to choose whether to follow the Lord's heavenly angels or whether to follow the now, unholy angels (fallen angels) who had power alongside God but rebelled against the Most High God.

130: What Happened After The Angels Rebelled?

It appears that Michael (archangel) remained true to God. He, with some of the other angels, drove Lucifer (Satan) and his followers (bad angels) from the third heaven. These evil angels have been in the natural heaven ever since.

131: How Long Will They Be In The Natural Heaven?

Lucifer isn't the prince of this world (II Cor. 4:4). He is the prince of the power of the air (Eph. 2:6). Amid the tribulation days, he and his unholy angels will be thrown down to the earth where he will have extraordinary fierceness. He will know he has just three and one-half years to work before he is thrown into the bottomless pit (Rev. 12). I would prefer not to be here around then. Prior to this time, the genuine holy angels will deliver me up to meet Jesus.

132: What Did The Fallen Angels Do Against God?

He attacked God's creation which was Adam and Eve. He wanted to rule over the universe which God had created. He tempted man to fall.

133: Do Evil Angels Attack Christians?

We wrestle against principalities (evil angels) and powers (evil angels) and against leaders of darkness (evil angels) in high places (Eph. 6:17). The weapons of our fighting are not fleshly but rather mighty through God to the pulling down of fortifications. You should utilize the weapons God has given you or be overwhelmed by evil angels.

134: Do Satan's Angels Hinder Us?

They hindered Jesus. Jesus sometimes had to pray all night. They hindered Paul from doing what he wanted to do (II Thess. 2:18). Paul fought with the beasts at Ephesus (I Cor. 15:32).

135: Is There An Angel Behind Each Ruler?

Since the devil has assembled every one of the legislatures (governments) together into a world government, he must have a agent through which to work. It is trusted that every leader of every country has an angel that goes with him to impact the issues of the countries.

We are directed to pray to God for the rulers. I supplicate that in this mindful position that one of God's blessed angels will be there; that the ruler will pursue directions of the right angel. Almost certainly there is a fight over the leaders of every national ruler. The great holy angels and the awful unholy evil angels are battling for control.

Daniel appeared to show us this reality when he said that one of Satan's angels was the ruler of the powers of Persia (Daniel 10:13). In somewhere else in the Scripture we locate that one of Satan's angels may have been relegated to run with the leader of a nation (Ezek. 28:12-19; Dan. 10:10-13;11:18).

136: Will Angels Help Bring In The Tribulation?

Truly, heavenly angels will free plagues upon the earth. They will be used to bring judgment (Rev. 15:17). They presently remain at the four quarters of the earth prepared to spill out the fierceness of God upon every corrupt man for the wicked deeds which they have ungodly committed.

137: What Are Some Of The Judgments The Angels Will Pour Out Upon The Ungodly Men Of Our Day?

One heavenly angel will make intolerable bruises break out upon men. Another heavenly angel will make the water in the oceans turn to blood. Another blessed angel will transform the waterways and wellsprings of water into blood. The fourth holy angel will make the sun be so hot it will sear men with flame. The fifth heavenly angel will make men chew their tongue with torment as a result of gross darkness. The 6th holy angel will cause the River Euphrates to be evaporated to plan for the clash of Armageddon.

There will be an extraordinary tremor (or earthquake). Each island will vanish. The mountains will vanish. Hail will fall weighing around one hundred pounds (Rev. 16). This is in the near future. What manner of person must we be. We should live so God's blessed angels will protect us as opposed to spilling out God's fury of his judgments. It is dependent upon you and me to exit under God's anger or God's benevolent mercy.

If we abide in this secret place of the Most High, we will give His heavenly angels charge over us to keep us in all our ways and no torment (plague) will come close to our dwelling (Psalm 91:10). Ten thousand will fall next to us, yet these plagues and judgments won't come near us. A heavenly angel is preferable protection over a man-made reinforced hideout.

138: Does Each Angel Have A Certain Duty To Perform In Judgment?

One holy angel will toss down flame blended with blood that will consume 33% of the trees and grass (Rev. 8:7). As one holy angel gives the signal one mountain consuming with flame and will make it fall into the sea, making 33% of it moved toward becoming blood (Rev. 8:9). As another gives a signal, he will make a consuming star fall making the water be severe, bitter. Another holy angel will put obscurity on the sun. One heavenly angel gives the signal and makes two hundred million of the fallen angel's messengers (evil angels) be turned free on the earth (Rev. 9; Joel 2).

One of these can take a city. They can't be murdered with a weapon. Men will want to die, however death will escape from them. Locust will sting men and they will languish over five months. They will attempt to die, however death will flee from them. One holy angel will fly through the earth and caution individuals. God's blessed angels will turn four powerful heavenly angels free and 33% of the men will bite the die.

139: Aren't These Angels Interested In Men?

They are concerned and keen on men. One of them will fly simply over the leaders of the general population and request that the general population acknowledge the gospel. It appears the judgments are to motivate men to repent. Anything is superior to anything being lost and going to an unending hell (Rev. 14:6). A heavenly angel will caution men not to take the mark of the beast. He will disclose to them that they will be lost, unsaved everlastingly in the event that they take this mark (Rev. 14:9).

140: Will An Angel Destroy Men?

A blessed angel will push in the sickle and harvest the earth (Rev. 14:19-20). Each man will die (Rev. 19:20,21). He will cast everything into the winepress of God's wrath. A horse can swim in human blood up to two hundred miles (Rev. 14:20). We,must be cautious consistently to remain on the triumphant side and not on the losing side. We should live so the holy angel will battle for us and not battle against us.

141: How Can We Tell When Angels Are Against Us?

If we are for the Lord, angels are for us. In the event that we are against the Lord, angels are against us. We are either for God or against God (Matt. 12:30). While Joshua was in fight, an invisible man was near him with a sword drawn (Joshua 5:13). Joshua's eyes were opened so he could see this invisible visitor. Maybe Joshua was the only one that saw him.

Joshua asked the man whose side he was on. The man said he was the commander of the Lord's hosts. He had a large group of blessed angels with him. It relied upon which side Joshua was battling. The heavenly angel was battling for Joshua, since Joshua was God's ally. Had he been on the wrong side, the holy angels would have battled against him. That is the reason we should make certain to remain on God's side.

142: Are Angels On Our Side?

They are on God's side. It is left up to us to be God's ally and they will battle for us. At the point when Peter was in jail, the congregation made petition for him. A holy angel came and let him out of jail (Acts 12:9).

143: Why Didn't King Herod Catch Peter, Put Him Back In Prison Or Kill Him?

A holy angel destroyed Herod and he was eaten with worms (Acts 12:23). If you don't serve God, If you don't give God the glory, the heavenly angel may turn to be your foe rather than your companion. Worms have eaten a great many individuals since they gave not God the glory. Quite a while prior, amid my pastorate, a evil woman endeavored to tear up the church. A heavenly angel protected me and destroyed her. Worms ate her. I'm happy I remained on the Lord's side.

144: Do Angels Believe In The Holy Bible?

God's holy angels are holy. The general population got the Bible by the administration of blessed angels (Acts 7:23). The Bible was appointed by holy angels in the hands of the mediator (Gal. 3:19). The words spoken by heavenly angels was steadfast so that each transgression (sin) and disobedience got a just recompense of reward (Heb. 2:2).

Heavenly angels will accompany Jesus to execute judgment upon those individuals who don't live according to the Bible (II Thess. 1:7,8).

145: Will Repentance Keep An Angel From Destroying You?

When a blessed angel began to devastate a whole city. David repented and made things ideal with God. The heavenly angel halted. The heavenly angel did not expedite judgments of God on the city (II Sam. 24:16). At the point when the judgments of God are going to fall on a country it is conceivable that our CEO could repent and call every one of us to prayer. The heavenly angel of judgment would stay his hand and our country would be spared a while longer.

146: Will An Angel Instruct Us How To Be Spared In Judgment?

A holy angel addressed the prophet of God and advised how to advise David to draw out the judgment (I Chron. 21:8). David fabricated a sacrificial table (altar) and the judgment was stayed. The sacrifice cost a huge cost. David declined to give a sacrifice to the Lord that cost him nothing.

For this situation the heavenly angel addressed the preacher rather than the CEO. David was withdrawn from the Lord around then. In the event that the president was not on talking terms with God, maybe a pastor of the gospel could be sent to the president.

Prayer

HEAVENLY FATHER, AS JUDGMENT is going to fall upon this country may you let the holy angel of God caution our CEO or a portion of the leaders; or send some pastor of the gospel to the CEO (the president). Master, judgment is going to fall on an individual since they are out of association with God.

Help them to do as David. Help them to bow their head, be modest, sacrifice and repent that you may remain the judgment, that you may drag out the judgment that is going to fall upon them. May you forgive them. May you heal their body and give them peace in their spirit, in Jesus' name and I will give you the praise.

Amen!

Bibliography

Ford, H. W. (1974) Great Christian Doctrines. Grand Rapids, MI.: Zondervan Publishing House.

Funk And Wagnalls Standard Dictionary Comprehensive. International Ed. Vol. I. Chicago, Ill.: J. G. Ferguson

Hyatt, P. J. (1964) The Heritage Of Biblical Faith. St. Louis, MO.: Bethany Press

Lindsay, G. (1972) Satan's Rebellion And Fall. Dallas, TX.: Christ For The Nations

New Combined Bible Dictionary And Concordance (1984). Dallas, TX.: American Evangelistic Association

White, E. G. (1988) The Great Controversy. Altamount, TN.: Harvest Time Press

Wiley, H. O. (1964) Christian Theology. Vols. 1 & 2. Kansas City, MO.: Beacon Hill Press

The Holy Bible (1964) Authorized King James Version. Chicago, Ill.: J. G. Ferguson

The Holy Bible (1953) The Revised Standard Version. Nashville, TN.: Thomas Nelson And Sons (Used By Permission)

The Holy Bible (1901) The American Standard Version. Nashville, Tn.: Thomas Nelson (Used By Permission)

The Holy Bible (1959) The Berkeley Version. Grand Rapids, MI.: Zondervan (Used By Permission)

The Holy Bible (2017) The New Testament Version. Grand Rapids, MI.: Zondervan (Used By Permission)

The New Testament In Modern English (1958) J. B. Philips, Macmillian (Used By Permission)

The New Testament In The Language Of The People (1937, 1949) Chicago, Ill.: Charles B. Williams, Bruce Humphries, Inc. Moody Bible Institute (Used By Permission)

About The Author

THE REVEREND DR. JOHN Thomas Wylie is one who has dedicated his life to the work of God's Service, the service of others; and being a powerful witness for the Gospel of Our Lord and Savior Jesus Christ. Dr. Wylie was called into the Gospel Ministry June 1979, whereby in that same year he entered The American Baptist College of the American Baptist Theological Seminary, Nashville, Tennessee.

As a young Seminarian, he read every book available to him that would help him better his understanding of God as well as God's plan of Salvation and the Christian Faith. He made a commitment as a promising student that he would inspire others as God inspires him. He understood early in his ministry that we live in times where people question not only who God is; but whether miracles are real, whether or not man can make a change, and who the enemy is or if the enemy truly exists.

Dr. Wylie carried out his commitment to God, which has been one of excellence which led to his earning his Bachelors of Arts in Bible/Theology/Pastoral Studies. Faithful and obedient to the call of God, he continued to matriculate in his studies earning his Masters of Ministry from Emmanuel Bible College, Nashville, Tennessee & Emmanuel Bible College, Rossville, Georgia. Still, inspired to please the Lord and do that which is well – pleasing in the Lord's sight, Dr. Wylie recently on March 2006, completed his Masters of Education degree with a concentration in Instructional Technology earned at The American Intercontinental University, Holloman Estates, Illinois. Dr. Wylie also previous to this, earned his Education

Specialist Degree from Jones International University, Centennial, Colorado and his Doctorate of Theology from The Holy Trinity College and Seminary, St. Petersburg, Florida.

Dr. Wylie has served in the capacity of pastor at two congregations in Middle Tennessee and Southern Tennessee, as well as served as an Evangelistic Preacher, Teacher, Chaplain, Christian Educator, and finally a published author, writer of many great inspirational Christian Publications such as his first publication: *"Only One God: Who Is He?" – published August 2002 via formally 1st books library (which is now AuthorHouse Book Publishers located in Bloomington, Indiana & Milton Keynes, United Kingdom)* which caught the attention of **The Atlanta Journal Constitution Newspaper.**

Dr. Wylie is happily married to Angel G. Wylie, a retired Dekalb Elementary School teacher who loves to work with the very young children and who always encourages her husband to move forward in the Name of Jesus Christ. They have Four children, 11 grand-children and one great-grandson of whom they are very proud. Both Dr. Wylie and Angela Wylie serve as members of the Salem Baptist Church, located in Lilburn, Georgia, where the Reverend Dr. Richard B. Haynes is Senior pastor.

Dr. Wylie has stated of his wife: "she knows the charm and beauty of sincerity, goodness, and purity through Jesus Christ. Yes, she is a Christian and realizes the true meaning of loveliness as the reflection as her life of holy living gives new meaning, hope, and purpose to that of her husband, her children, others may say of her, "Behold the handmaiden of the Lord." A Servant of Jesus Christ!

About The Book

IN THIS PUBLICATION, "ANGELS And Spirits," the Scripture teaches that there is an order of intelligences higher than that of men; and further asserts that these intelligences are connected with man in providence and in the redemptive economy. These intelligences are called "Spirits" to denote their specific role and nature; they are called "Angels" to denote their mission. We will investigate their involvement with mankind and their tasks. Nothing can be known of them other than that which is revealed in the Scriptures. They are created spirits but the time of their creation is not indicated. Many Biblical Scholars hold that such a creation must have been included in the statement found in Genesis 1:1, and therefore preceding the six days' formative period.

The highest exercise of angels is to wait upon God. Their chief duty is to minister to the heirs of salvation. As we embark upon this reading, my hope is that you will come to take seriously the informative topics presented to you. We do not intend to dwell on Satan or his angels too much (only as necessary), but focus on the deeds and tasks of holy angels.

Reverend Dr. John Thomas Wylie